W9-CDF-979

Organize Your Life

Organize Your Life

Securely Archive Your Important Family Records

Abigail Wilentz

The Reader's Digest Association, Inc.
Pleasantville, New York/Montreal/London

A READER'S DIGEST BOOK

This edition published by The Reader's Digest Association, Inc, by arrangement with Ilex Press Limited.

This book was conceived, designed, and produced by:
The Ilex Press, 210 High Street, Lewes, BN7 2NS, UK

FOR ILEX PRESS
Publisher Alastair Campbell
Creative Director Peter Bridgewater
Associate Publisher Adam Juniper
Managing Editors Chris Gatcum, Natalia Price-Cabrera
Senior Designer James Hollywell
Designer Ginny Zeal

FOR READER'S DIGEST
U.S. Project Editor Kim Casey
Manager, English Book Editorial, Reader's Digest Canada Pamela Johnson
Canadian Project Editors Jesse Corbeil, J. D. Gravenor
Project Designer Jennifer Tokarski
Senior Art Director George McKeon
Executive Editor, Trade Publishing Dolores York
Associate Publisher, Trade Publishing Rosanne McManus
President and Publisher, Trade Publishing Harold Clarke

LIBRARY OF CONGRESS CATALOGING-IN-PUBLICATION DATA
Wilentz, Abigail, 1970-
Organize your life ; securely archive your important family records / Abigail Wilentz.
p. cm.
Includes index.
ISBN 978-1-60652-148-9
1. Family records--Management--Data processing. 2. Information storage and retrieval systems--Archival materials. 3. Electronic filing systems. I. Reader's Digest Association. II. Title.
HF5736.W737 2010
640--dc22
2010015866

We are committed to both the quality of our products and the service we provide to our customers. We value your comments, so please feel free to contact us.

The Reader's Digest Association, Inc.
Adult Trade Publishing
Westchester One, 18th floor
44 S. Broadway, White Plains, NY 10601

For more Reader's Digest products and information, visit our website:
www.rd.com (in the United States)
www.readersdigest.ca (in Canada)
www.readersdigest.co.uk (in the UK)

Printed in and bound in China
1 3 5 7 9 10 8 6 4 2

PHOTO CREDITS
iStockphoto.com
6, 8–10, 12B, 14L, 15, 16B, 17, 25, 26C, 29, 46TL, 54BL, 59, 64–65, 144TL, 145BL, 162R, 164TL

Fotolia
2–3, 12TL, 14TL, 16TL, 22TL, 24TL, 26R, 27, 28TL, 30TL, 32TL, 34TL, 36TL, 38TL, 42TL, 44TL, 50TL, 54TL, 56TL, 58TL, 60TL, 63

CONTENTS

Introduction 6

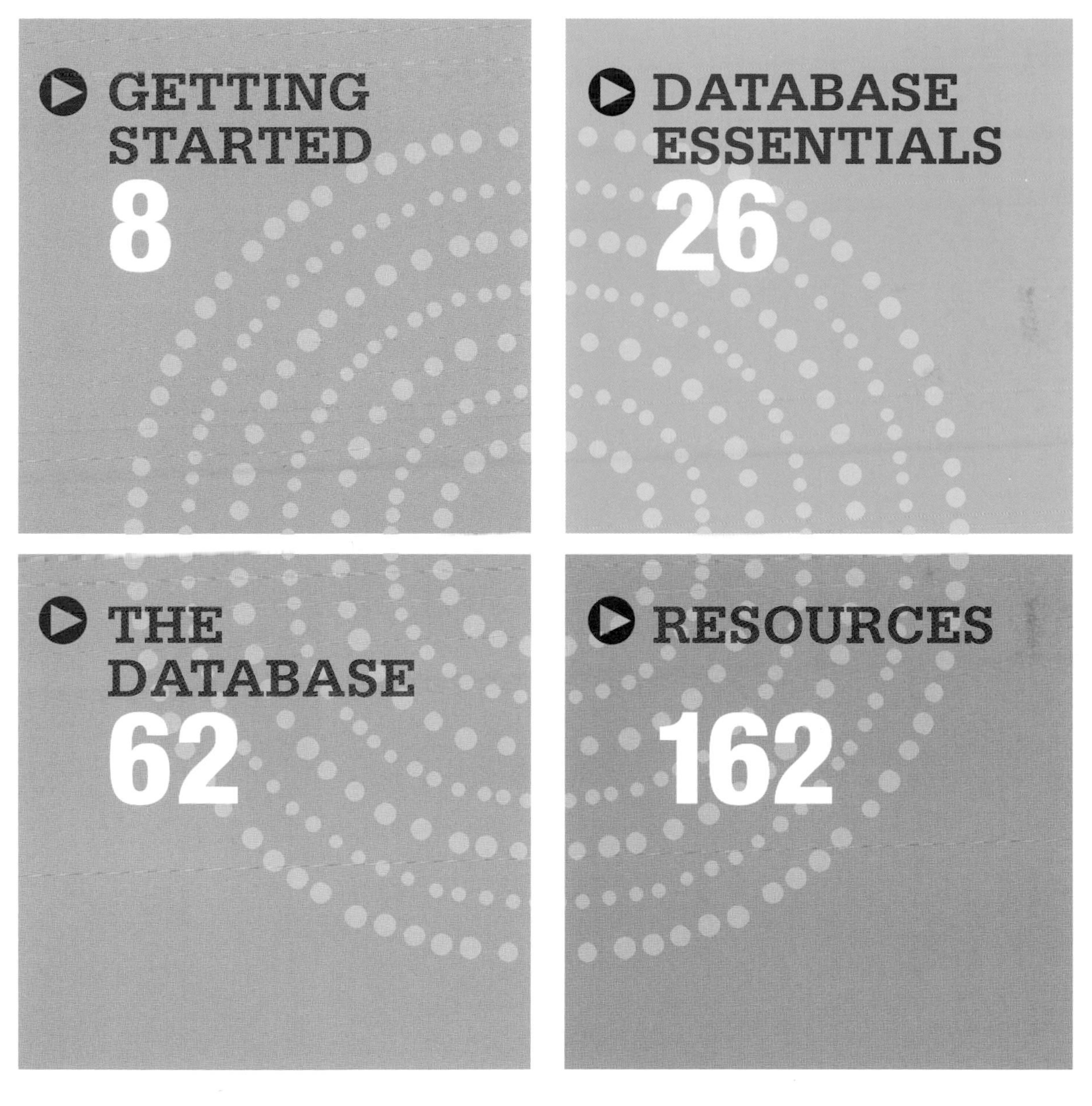

Troubleshooting 164
Glossary 170
Index 174

Introduction

Wave good-bye to drawers stuffed with old paperwork, messy piles of paper, and important information kept on the back of an old envelope. *Organize Your Life* will revolutionize the way you store personal data.

If you start to think about how much data you collect in your everyday life, you will soon realize that there is a sizeable amount of information about yourself, your family, your home, your cars, your investments, and so on that you need to keep safe and accessible. Much of this will likely be stored in a single location—a personal filing cabinet, for example—and while no one wants to think that disasters will happen to them, what if they did?

What if your home caught fire or it was flooded? Apart from the loss of personal treasures and items of sentimental value, how would you get back on your feet again? How easily could you retrieve copies of important documents, such as birth or marriage certificates, or warranties for household goods, if the originals were lost? If you wanted to make an insurance claim, do you have a list of all your valuables, do you have receipts, and do you know their current value? You may have jewelry or antiques, but do you have photographs that might aid in their recovery if they were stolen, or at the very least enable you to claim for their full value?

Unfortunately this is not something that most people consider until it is too late, but it doesn't have to be like that. The computer program that accompanies this book is the ideal solution, because it allows you to store all your vital personal records in a single location that is easily accessible, secure, and, most important, is in a format that can be duplicated for safe storage.

Whether you need to locate a copy of your birth certificate or find something as trivial as your dentist's telephone number, all the data you might need to access can be stored on your computer, allowing you to wave good-bye to drawers stuffed with old paperwork, messy piles of paper, and important telephone numbers written on the back of an old envelope. In addition, you will have the peace of mind that, if the worst should happen, you will be able to access all your vital information with just a couple of clicks of your mouse.

SHARES
CREDIT DOCUMENTS
HOUSE INSURANCE
MORTGAGE
PASSPORT

GETTING STARTED

In this chapter you will learn the basics of how the *Organize Your Life* program works and the type of information you will be able to store in it. Much of this information you will already have on hand, but some you may need to research, whether that means digging it out from your file cabinet or locating it online.

Once you have gathered your records, facts, photos, and more, you will want to enter them into the program. So this book will talk you through how to scan your documents and photographs to get the best results. You will also learn the appropriate file types for documents and images. Once you have digitized your documents, you want to be sure they are properly saved for future accessibility, so you'll never have to spend time searching again.

How the Program Works

Organize Your Life is a database, and in many ways it's like a digital filing cabinet, allowing you to store information within a very systematic structure. However, unlike a filing cabinet, a database is much neater, and it's much easier to retrieve the information you need.

Since the database is on your computer, and because it's in a digital format, it has a number of advantages over a traditional filing cabinet. It's much easier to search for a specific term in a database than it is to go through a pile of paperwork by hand, and you can add far more information to a database without it becoming disorganized. It may be easy to file paperwork, but as the amount of paper increases, you not only need more storage space, it also becomes more difficult and time consuming to find anything—even if you are organized.

Database benefits

However, this doesn't apply to a database. It will sit neatly on your computer, where the only space it takes up is space on your computer's hard drive—and it won't use much of that. More importantly, you can enter far more information. It can be simple entries, such as names, dates, addresses, and phone numbers, or more extensive descriptions about property, valuables, or personal notes on members of your family. It also allows you to upload documents and photographs, so all the information you need to have handy is in a single location.

In addition, everything you enter into the database can be updated and changed whenever needed. For example, if you move to a new house, you can quickly and easily update all of your utility records, as well as find the names and addresses of the companies you need to contact with your change of address. And you can do all of this without having to unpack boxes of paperwork and bills!

It's easy to fill a filing cabinet with paperwork. However, the more you save, the harder it is to find a specific document at a later date. With a digital database it's much easier to search for the information you need.

Key Database Terminology

Before you look at the database in more detail, here are a few fundamental database terms:

Record

When you add a new job to your list of employment, for example, or a doctor's visit to your medical history, you are adding a new record. Basically a record contains all the information you have entered on a particular individual or event, place, or thing.

Field

Each record allows you to enter specific information in subcategories—descriptive facts such as name, date, address, and so on. Each of these subcategories in a record is known as a field.

Record ID

A unique ID number is assigned to each record in case the information entered in one record reappears in others within the database. This way, each record is discrete from all others, regardless of the information it contains, and is easy to locate.

Each page of the database program is a record.

A record contains a number of places where you can enter information—each of these data entry points is a field.

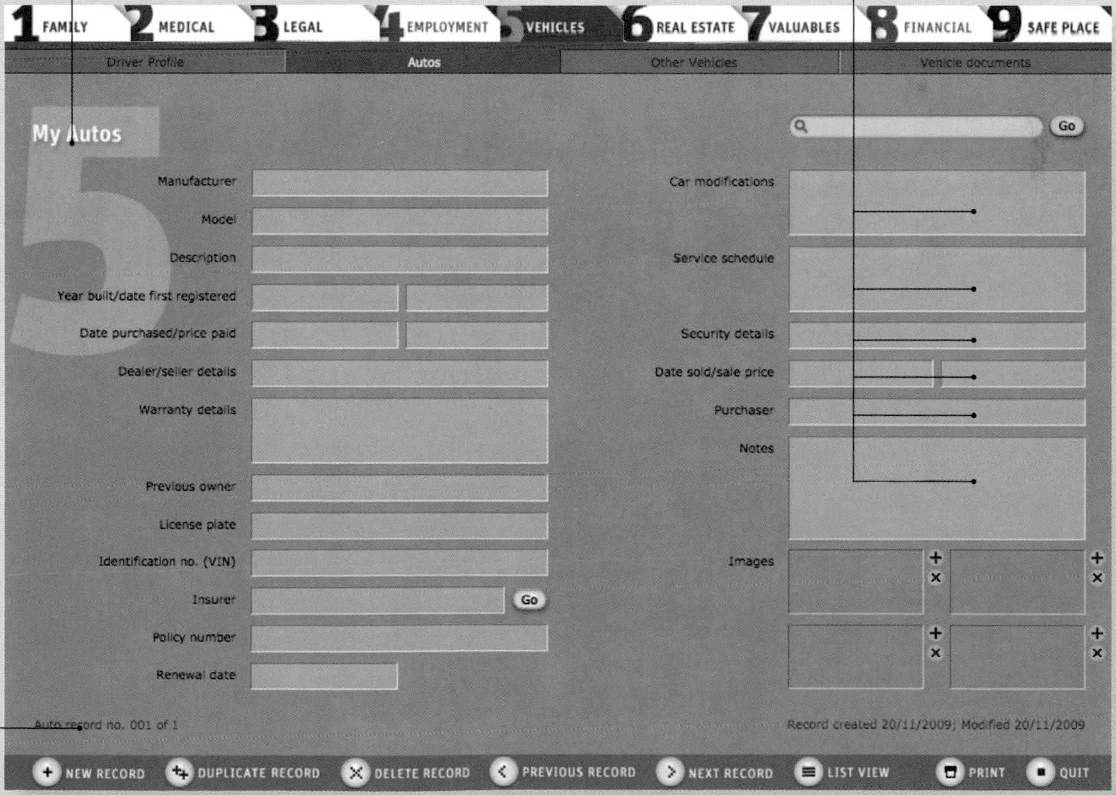

Every record has its own record ID number assigned automatically, so each one is unique.

What Records Can You Store?

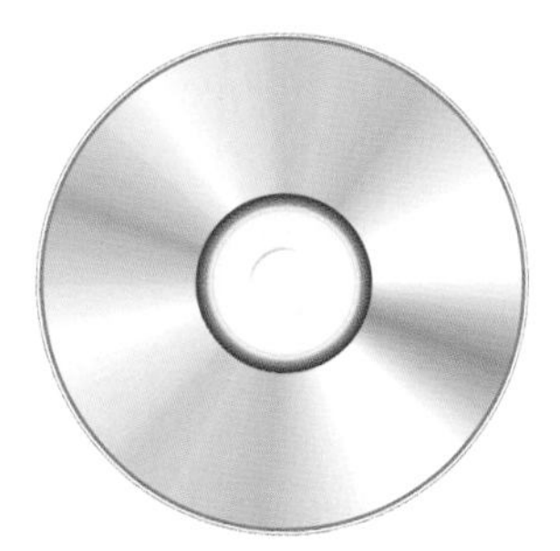

The *Organize Your Life* program is unique in the breadth of information it allows you to store. By using this single database, you will be able to keep all your important documentation and details in one place—from family, medical, legal, and employment, to vehicles, valuables, and financial information.

Each of these areas is broken down to offer you the maximum potential opportunity for inputting pertinent information: The financial section, for example, has records covering everything from your bank accounts and credit cards, to your pension, taxes, and life insurance. In the property section, you can enter the contact and account information for all the companies you use to manage the upkeep of your home: gas, oil, electricity, cable, and telephone. Similarly the medical records' section gives you a place to list your doctors' contact information, the dates of any visits and the corresponding prognoses, plus descriptions of medical conditions, prescriptions, allergies, dietary restrictions, and so on.

In fact, the database lets you save all the practical details that are useful to have at your fingertips, and you can choose to fill in as much—or as little—information as you like. You will certainly find that the more you add, the more you will easily arrange the growing pile of paperwork that can overwhelm your daily life.

Storing your records in a database means you can access them quickly and easily, rather than hunting through filing cabinets.

Records at a Glance

Organize Your Life allows you to store a wide variety of information. Here's a quick rundown of the nine sections, and the record pages you will find within them:

Where to Find Your Records

You probably already have easy access to many of the records you'll want to enter in the program—and chances there are even more than you realize. For most people, the start—and possibly end—of the search will be a filing cabinet where you store all your printed personal information.

All contact information for your work usually appears on your business card or letterhead; your passport number is printed in your passport; your doctors' and lawyers' contact information will be on their receipts or bills sent to you by mail. If you rent your home or apartment, the management company's information will be on your monthly bills. And if you purchased your residence from a realtor or estate agent, the paperwork from the sale includes all the necessary information.

Running your home generates a vast amount of paperwork, so it's time to get organized.

Residence

If you are maintaining your residence, you are billed by your local gas, oil, and electricity companies as well as telephone, cable, and other services depending on your lifestyle—from pool maintenance to landscapers, and so on. So if you have any bills, you will have no trouble accessing the information you need for these.

Car

For information on your car, the paperwork from your purchase or leasing agreement will provide all you need—if you have questions, simply call the dealership.

If you regularly book international flights online you will be asked for your passport number, so it is useful to have it stored in the database for reference.

Bills and receipts will provide you with a lot of information about your utility companies and suppliers—from your account number to their contact details.

Finances

Regarding taxes, you should have copies of your tax returns, which show your yearly income and taxes paid. If you don't have these on hand, your accountant will certainly be able to provide the necessary details.

In terms of personal finances, your bank account details, as well as credit card information, are included in your monthly statements, or you can find the information online, if you've signed up for online banking services. Similarly if you have investments, such as stocks or bonds, you will be receiving periodic statements from the investment firm.

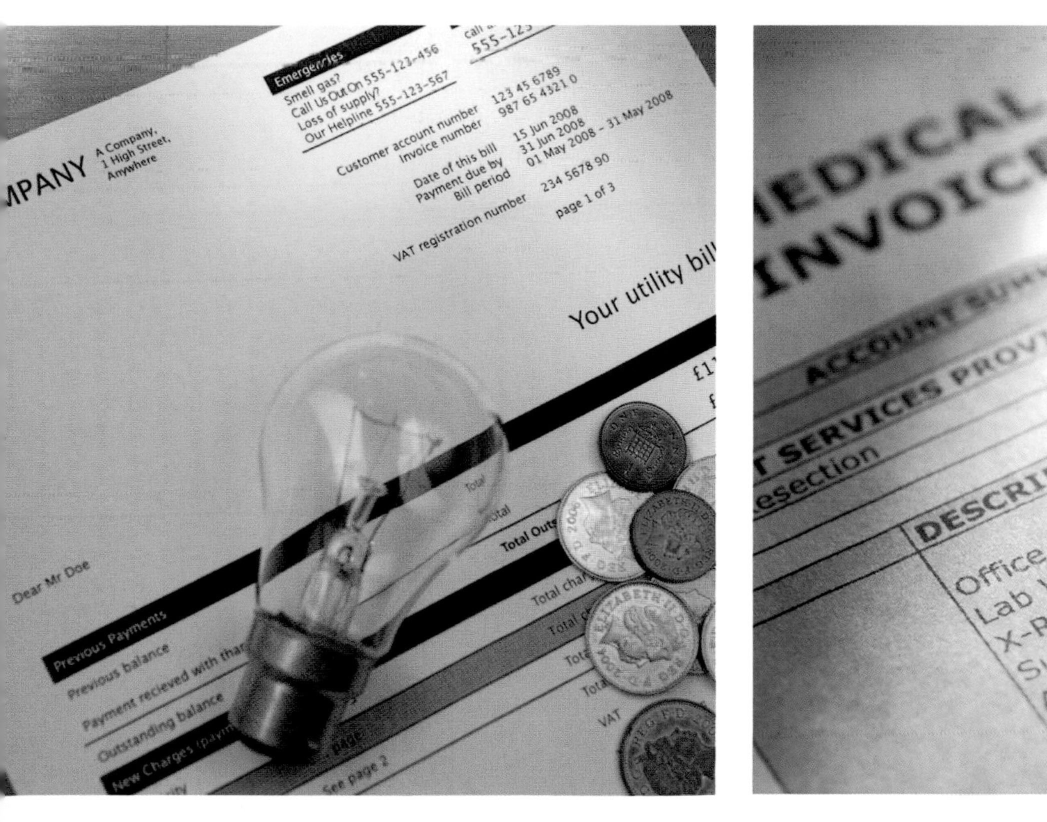

If You Are Missing Records

If you find that you are missing some of the records you need, in most cases it is not difficult to recover them. For medical, financial, legal, and many other personal records, you can directly contact the office that generated this information, whether it's your doctor, lawyer, accountant, or stockbroker.

In many cases today, however, you may also be able to locate the information you need online. Certainly you can access all your bank account information: All you will need is a user name and password, and you can check your banking records 24 hours a day, going back over a period of months or even years. The same is true when you want to locate records of your pension plan and investments, such as stocks and shares. Once you are set up with an account, you can monitor their activity as well as make changes as you see fit.

Your doctor will hold your medical records, so if you need to find out something from your medical history, contacting the medical office is a good place to start.

Medical

Many health plans allow you to access your health insurance over the Internet, so you can view details of your plan, as well as submit claims and check the status of any payments. If you take prescription medications long term, you may be able to order them online instead of purchasing them at your local pharmacy. The online service will keep track of your prescription records, such as what medications are prescribed by which doctor, when to order refills, and when they expire.

In general, signing up for online accounts is a great way to start reducing the endless clutter of paper statements, and it is the ideal way to begin your search for the information you want to add to your personal records database.

If you have signed up for online banking, it is easy to find all the bank account information you need for the database.

Avoid Phishing

Although it is easy to conduct most of your day-to-day personal business online, the last thing you want is for anyone to get hold of your personal information—especially your bank account details. A common scam is phishing, where you receive an e-mail from someone claiming to be your bank. This is simply an attempt to get your personal banking details, so:

- **NEVER** share your online banking password and security information with anyone, and **NEVER** have it written down. If someone finds it, they can immediately access your bank account from any computer.
- If you receive an e-mail claiming to be from your bank, which asks for your account details and password, **DO NOT** send them. Most, if not all, banks will never e-mail such a request.
- If you receive an e-mail asking you to click a link to "update your security details," **DO NOT** click on it. The website it takes you to might *look* like your bank's, but it might not be real. Website styles are easy to copy. Even if the linked website is clearly a fake when you open it, chances are it may already have downloaded a virus onto your computer.
- If you ever receive an e-mail purporting to be from your bank that you aren't sure about, **ALWAYS** contact your bank by telephone to determine whether it is genuine or not.

Scanning on a Windows PC

A scanner is a useful tool for converting your printed documents and photographs into digital form, so you can use them on your computer. Once they have been scanned, you can add both photographs and copies of documents to your records in the database program.

Because the process for scanning a photo and scanning a document is essentially the same, there is only one set of instructions here. The process might vary depending on your specific scanner model and your computer's operating system. If you are using a Mac, there are separate instructions on page 20.

Check that your scanner is connected to your computer and the power is on. Next place your document or photograph facedown in the scanner, so the top left corner rests in the corner of the scanner marked with the arrow.

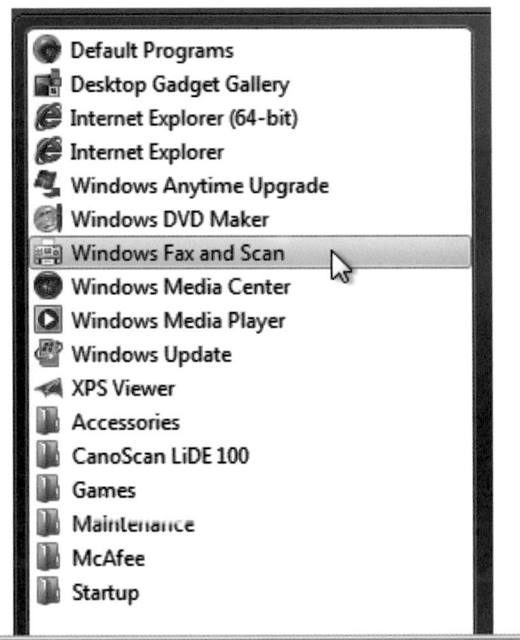

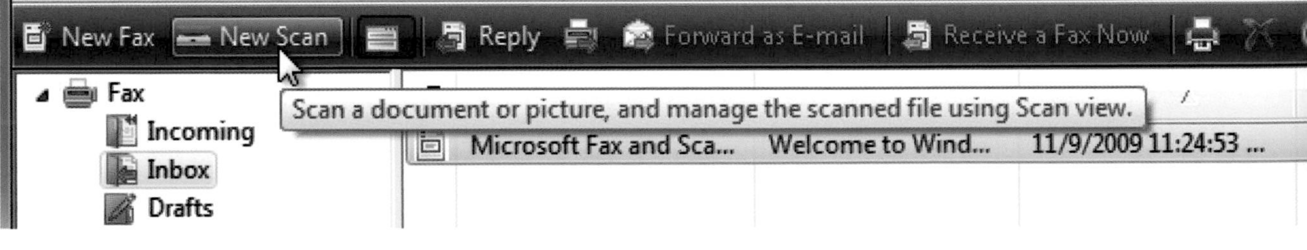

1 Launch the Windows *Fax and Scan* tool by clicking on the *Start* button and selecting *Windows Fax and Scan* from the *Programs* menu.

2 The window might appear to be oriented around functionality, but don't worry about it. Choose the *New Scan* button from the toolbar.

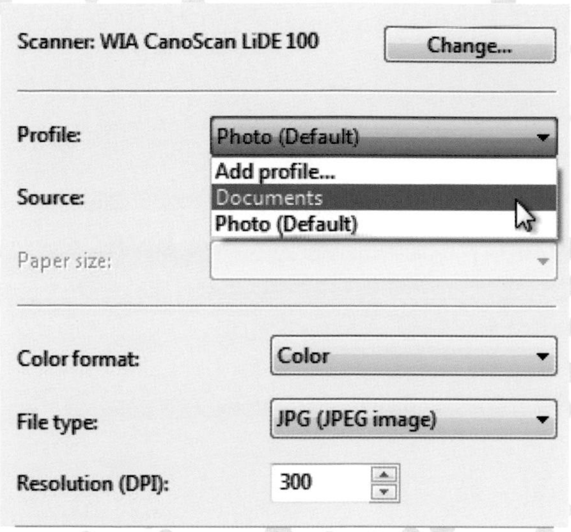

Scanner: WIA CanoScan LiDE 100 Change...

Profile: Photo (Default)
Add profile...
Documents
Photo (Default)

Source:

Paper size:

Color format: Color

File type: JPG (JPEG image)

Resolution (DPI): 300

❸ Select the *Documents* mode from the *New Scan* dialog box (or *Photo* if you are scanning a photograph). If your document has any color elements, select *Color*; if not, choose *Black and White* in the *Color* format dialog. Next set the file type—to JPEG or PDF for documents or JPEG for photographs. Finally, set the resolution. You'll find that 300 ppi (or "dpi," depending on your scanner's terminology) is more than adequate for both photographs and documents. Once you've made these adjustments, click *Preview*.

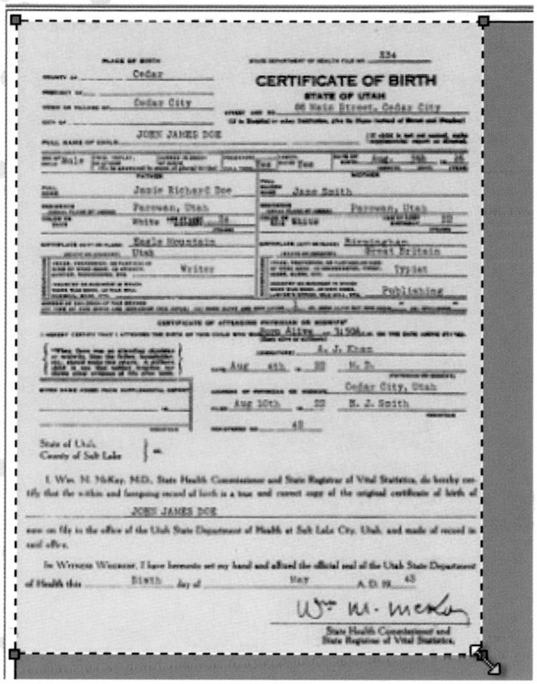

CERTIFICATE OF BIRTH
STATE OF UTAH
Cedar
Cedar City
JOHN JAMES DOE
Jamie Richard Doe
Parowan, Utah
Jane Smith
Eagle Mountain
Birmingham
Great Britain
Writer
Typist
Publishing
A. J. Khan
Aug 4th
Cedar City, Utah
Aug 10th
H. J. Smith
State of Utah
County of Salt Lake
JOHN JAMES DOE

❹ The scanner will now make a low-resolution preview of the entire scan area with a dotted crop box around it. You need to adjust the scan area to the edges of your document or photo, so click and drag the lower right corner of the crop box so the rectangle tightly fits around the page.

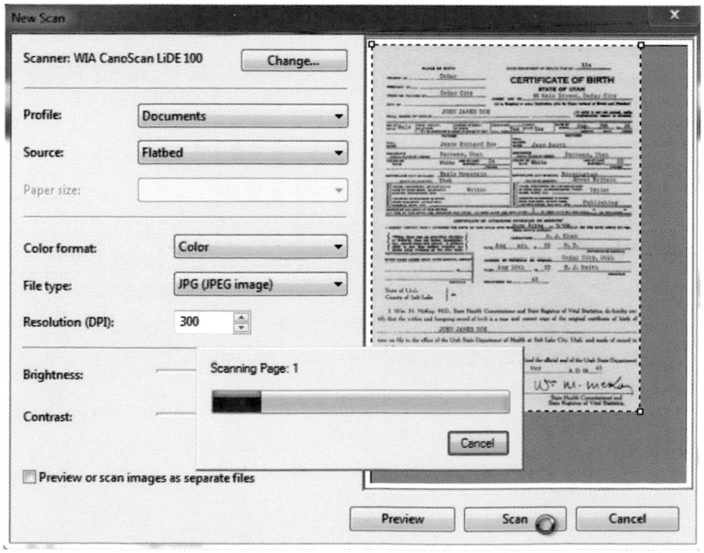

New Scan

Scanner: WIA CanoScan LiDE 100 Change...

Profile: Documents

Source: Flatbed

Paper size:

Color format: Color

File type: JPG (JPEG image)

Resolution (DPI): 300

Brightness:

Contrast:

Scanning Page: 1

Cancel

Preview or scan images as separate files

Preview Scan Cancel

❺ Once you have set the crop, click the *Scan* button to make your final scan. You will be returned to the Windows *Fax and Scan* screen with your scanned document (or photograph) visible. If you are using Windows 7, the scan will be saved in the *Libraries> Documents>Scanned Documents* directory on your computer's hard drive.

Scanning on a Mac

One of the easiest ways to access your scanner using a Mac is to use the *Image Capture* program that comes with the computer's operating system. The following steps are based on Mac OS X 10.6 (Snow Leopard) and might vary if you have an earlier version of the operating system.

You can check which operating system you are using by clicking on the *Apple* icon at the top left of the screen and then choose *About This Mac*.

The next thing you need to do is to make sure your scanner is connected to your computer and is switched on. Then load your document (or photograph) into the scanner. Once this is done, you are ready to make your scan.

1 Launch the *Image Capture* program. If this isn't on your dock, the quickest way to find the program is to click on the *Spotlight* icon in the upper right corner of the screen and type image capture in the search box. The program *Image Capture* is likely to be the top hit—just click on the name to start the program.

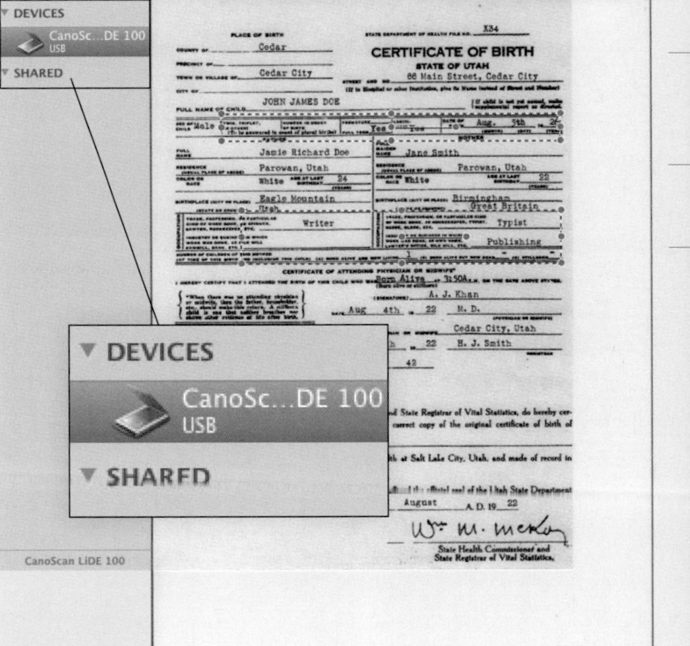

2 Select your scanner from the *Devices* list on the left. Your scanner will automatically conduct a preview scan. If it appears correct, click the *Show Details* button; if not, lift the lid and reposition the document or photograph as necessary.

PLACE OF BIRTH

STATE DEPARTMENT OF HEALTH FILE NO. X34

COUNTY OF Cedar

PRECINCT OF

TOWN OR VILLAGE OF Cedar City

CITY OF

CERTIFICATE OF BIRTH

STATE OF UTAH

STREET AND NO. 86 Main Street, Cedar City

(If in Hospital or other Institution, give its Name instead of Street and Number)

FULL NAME OF CHILD JOHN JAMES DOE

SEX OF CHILD Male — PREMATURE — FULL TERM Yes — LEGITIMATE Yes — DATE OF BIRTH Aug. 5th 19 26

FATHER		MOTHER	
FULL NAME	Jamie Richard Doe	FULL MAIDEN NAME	Jane Smith
RESIDENCE (USUAL PLACE OF ABODE)	Parowan, Utah	RESIDENCE (USUAL PLACE OF ABODE)	Parowan, Utah
COLOR OR RACE	White — AGE AT LAST BIRTHDAY 24 (YEARS)	COLOR OR RACE	White — AGE AT LAST BIRTHDAY 22 (YEARS)
BIRTHPLACE (CITY OR PLACE)	Eagle Mountain	BIRTHPLACE (CITY OR PLACE)	Birmingham
(STATE OR COUNTRY)	Utah	(STATE OR COUNTRY)	Great Britain
OCCUPATION: TRADE, PROFESSION, OR PARTICULAR KIND OF WORK DONE	Writer	OCCUPATION: TRADE, PROFESSION, OR PARTICULAR KIND OF WORK DONE	Typist
INDUSTRY OR BUSINESS IN WHICH WORK WAS DONE		INDUSTRY OR BUSINESS IN WHICH WORK WAS DONE	Publishing

NUMBER OF CHILDREN OF THIS MOTHER (AT TIME OF THIS BIRTH AND INCLUDING THIS CHILD) (A) BORN ALIVE AND NOW LIVING 1 (B) BORN ALIVE BUT NOW DEAD — (C) STILLBORN —

CERTIFICATE OF ATTENDING PHYSICIAN OR MIDWIFE*

I HEREBY CERTIFY THAT I ATTENDED THE BIRTH OF THIS CHILD WHO WAS Born Alive (Born alive or stillborn) AT 3:50A.M. ON THE DATE ABOVE STATED.

*When there was no attending physician or midwife, then the father, householder, etc., should make this return. A stillborn child is one that neither breathes nor shows other evidence of life after birth.

(SIGNATURE) A. J. Khan

DATE Aug 4th 19 22 M. D. (PHYSICIAN OR MIDWIFE)

GIVEN NAME ADDED FROM SUPPLEMENTAL REPORT

ADDRESS OF PHYSICIAN OR MIDWIFE Cedar City, Utah

FILED Aug 10th 19 22 H. J. Smith REGISTRAR

REGISTERED NO. 42

State of Utah, County of Salt Lake } ss.

I, Wm. M. McKay, M.D., State Health Commissioner and State Registrar of Vital Statistics, do hereby certify that the within and foregoing record of birth is a true and correct copy of the original certificate of birth of

DAVID EDWARDS

now on file in the office of the Utah State Department of Health at Salt Lake City, Utah, and made of record in said office.

In Witness Whereof, I have hereunto set my hand and affixed the official seal of the Utah State Department of Health this Twelth day of August A.D. 19 22

Wm. M. McKay

State Health Commissioner and State Registrar of Vital Statistics.

PLACE OF BIRTH

STATE DEPARTMENT OF HEALTH FILE NO. X34

COUNTY OF Cedar

TOWN OR VILLAGE OF Cedar City

CERTIFICATE OF BIRTH

STATE OF UTAH

STREET AND NO. 86 Main Street, Cedar City

FULL NAME OF CHILD JOHN JAMES DOE

Male Yes Yes Aug. 5th 26

Jamie Richard Doe — Jane Smith

Parowan, Utah — Parowan, Utah

White 24 — White 22

Eagle Mountain, Utah — Birmingham, Great Britain

Writer — Typist, Publishing

Born Alive 3:50A.M.

A. J. Khan

Aug 4th 22 M. D.

Cedar City, Utah

Aug 10th 22 H. J. Smith

42

State of Utah, County of Salt Lake } ss.

I, Wm. M. McKay, M.D., State Health Commissioner and State Registrar of Vital Statistics, do hereby certify that the within and foregoing record of birth is a true and correct copy of the original certificate of birth of

DAVID EDWARDS

now on file in the office of the Utah State Department of Health at Salt Lake City, Utah, and made of record in said office.

In Witness Whereof, I have hereunto set my hand and affixed the official seal of the Utah State Department of Health this Twelth day of August A.D. 19 22

State Health Commissioner and State Registrar of Vital Statistics.

3 The scanning software will attempt to automatically locate the edges of your document, but it can be confused by forms with wide white borders. If this happens, uncheck the *Detect Separate Items* button in the options and you will be left with only one outlined area on your preview.

4 Click inside the outlined area so round handles appear around the outside. Click and drag the handles to the area you want to scan.

Image Capture

DEVICES

CanoScan DE 100

SHARED

Kind: Color

Colors: Millions

Resolution: 300 dpi

Size: 17.88 23.80 cm

Rotation Angle: 0°

Detect Separate Items

Scan To: Pictures

Name: John Birth Certificate

Format: JPEG

Image Correction: None

Hide Details — Overview — Cancel

5 Adjust the resolution setting to 300 dpi, then select a name and save location for the file in the *Scan To* field. Finally choose an appropriate file type for the scan—JPEG for pictures and JPEG or PDF for documents—and click *Scan*. The file will be scanned and saved, ready to be included in your records database.

Optimizing Your Scans

Although your scans will often come out as you expect, there will be occasions when they do not. The most common problem is a document or photograph that has not been inserted into the scanner perfectly straight. However, you may also find that the resulting image lacks contrast.

There are ways to correct both of these problems, and in this case the solution uses the popular image-editing program Adobe Photoshop Elements. You can use a different program if you have one, such as Corel's Paint Shop Pro, but if not, you can download a free 30-day tryout from www.adobe.com.

If you use Elements, the first step is to choose the *Edit* mode and then open your image using the *File>Open* command. If you are using Windows 7, you will find the scan you made in the *Libraries>Documents>Scanned Documents* directory. If you are using a Mac, it will be in the location you specified when you made the scan.

STRAIGHTENING AN IMAGE

1. If you find that your scan is slightly uneven, choose the *Straighten* tool from the toolbox. This tool allows you to indicate a line that should be horizontal or vertical—such as the edge of the page—and the computer will rotate the scan accordingly.

2. Locate a straight line and click once at the left (or top) of it. You will notice a line appears between this point and wherever you move the mouse. Carefully position the mouse at the other end of your guideline—the longer it is, the more accurate your rotation will be. Click the mouse again and the scan will instantly be rotated.

Solid Color...
Gradient...
Pattern...
Levels...
Brightness/Contrast...
Hue/Saturation...
Gradient Map...
Photo Filter...
Invert
Threshold...
Posterize...

RACE White BIRTHDAY (YEARS) | RACE White
BIRTHPLACE (CITY OR PLACE) Eagle Mountain (STATE OR COUNTRY) Utah | BIRTHPLACE (CITY OR PLACE) Birmingham (STATE OR COUNTRY) Great B
OCCUPATION TRADE, PROFESSION, OR PARTICULAR KIND OF WORK DONE, AS SPINNER, SAWYER, BOOKKEEPER, ETC. Writer | TRADE, PROFESSION, OR PARTICULAR KIND OF WORK DONE, AS HOUSEKEEPER, TYPIST, NURSE, CLERK, ETC. Typist
INDUSTRY OR BUSINESS IN WHICH WORK WAS DONE, AS SILK MILL, SAWMILL, BANK, ETC. | INDUSTRY OR BUSINESS IN WHICH WORK WAS DONE, AS OWN HOME, LAWYER'S OFFICE, SILK MILL, ETC. Publishing
NUMBER OF CHILDREN OF THIS MOTHER (AT TIME OF THIS BIRTH AND INCLUDING THIS CHILD) (A) BORN ALIVE AND NOW LIVING 1 (B) BORN ALIVE BUT NOW DEAD – (C) STILLBORN –

CERTIFICATE OF ATTENDING PHYSICIAN OR MIDWIFE*
I HEREBY CERTIFY THAT I ATTENDED THE BIRTH OF THIS CHILD WHO WAS Born Alive AT 3:50A.M. ON THE DATE ABOVE STATED.
(Born alive or stillborn)
*When there was no attending physician or midwife, then the father, householder, etc., should make this return. A stillborn child is one that neither breathes nor shows other evidence of life after birth.
(SIGNATURE) A. J. Khan
DATE Aug 4th 22 M. D.
GIVEN NAME ADDED FROM SUPPLEMENTAL REPORT
ADDRESS OF PHYSICIAN
FILED Aug 10th
REGISTRAR
REGISTERED NO.

State of Utah,
County of Salt Lake } ss.

I, Wm. M. McKay, M.D., State Health Commissioner and S[...] tify that the within and foregoing record of birth is a true and co[...]
JOHN JAMES DOE
now on file in the office of the Utah State Department of Health [...] said office.
In Witness Whereof, I have hereunto set my hand and affix[...] of Health this Sixth day of

RGB
37 1.00 255
Output Levels: 0 255

ADJUSTING THE CONTRAST

1 Increasing the contrast is especially useful in a document to make sure that the paper appears white and the text looks black, but it is also useful for photographs, too. The best solution is a *Levels* adjustment. Locate the *Layers* panel and click on the *Create new fill or adjustment layer* button, which appears as a circle—half black, half white. Choose *Levels* from the pop-up menu.

2 In the *Levels* pane that appears, there is a graphic representation of the contrast of your scan: Dark tones appear as peaks near the left, light tones at the right. In this example, the text should be black, but it has scanned as a dark gray. To solve this problem, click on the black triangle beneath the histogram and slide it to the right until it touches the edge of the graph.

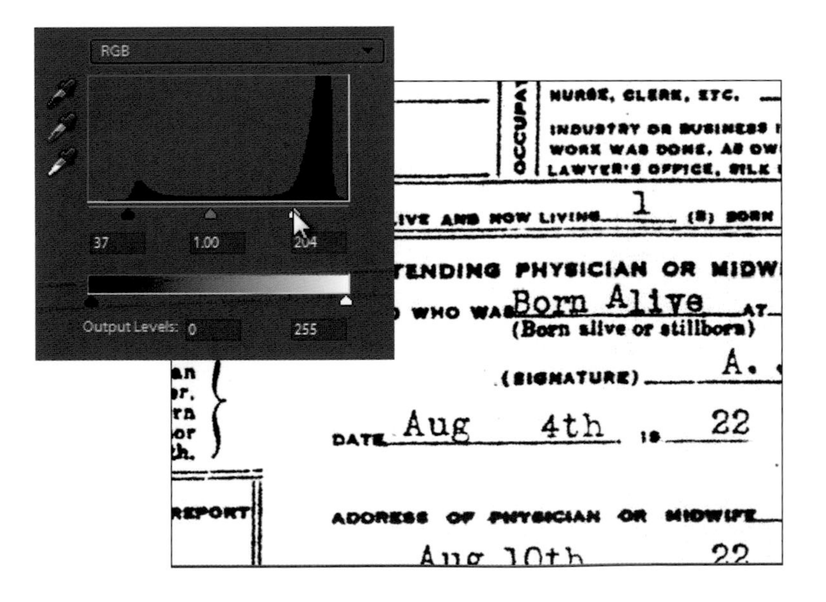

3 At the other end of the scale, there is a large spike in the light area; it's not against the edge but a little way in, so it must represent the paper, which has not come out in the scan as white. To fix this, drag the white triangle beneath the graph to the left so that all the paper appears to be clean white.

4 Once you've made your contrast adjustments, and you are happy that the paper is white and the text is black, you can save the corrected file using the *File>Save As* option.

Saving Files

There are many digital file types, and they all store information in different ways. It's easy to get confused by all the file types and their extensions, but for the purpose of the database, you need only be concerned with two of them: PDF files for documents and JPEG files for images.

PDF

Short for Portable Document Format, a PDF file will save all of a document's original elements—such as the text, graphics, layout, and font. Many companies now send PDF files when you request electronic versions of documents, such as auto insurance records, because PDF files can be opened even if the person they are sent to does not have the original program in which the document was created, or has a computer with a different operating system. This is because the only program you need to open and read a PDF file is Adobe Acrobat Reader, which is a free download from Adobe (www.adobe.com), who originally developed the PDF format. PDFs are fully compatible with the database program you will be using to store your personal records, and they are a good format for documents you want to scan and include.

John Birth Certificate.pdf - Adobe Reader

File Edit View Document Tools Window Help

John Birth Certificate.pdf

PLACE OF BIRTH

STATE DEPARTMENT OF HEALTH FILE NO. X34

CERTIFICATE OF BIRTH

STATE OF UTAH

COUNTY OF Cedar

PRECINCT OF

TOWN OR VILLAGE OF Cedar City

CITY OF

STREET AND NO. 66 Main Street, Cedar City

(If in Hospital or other Institution, give its Name instead of Street and Number)

FULL NAME OF CHILD JOHN JAMES DOE

(If child is not yet named, make supplemental report as directed.

SEX OF CHILD Male | TWIN, TRIPLET, OR OTHER? | NUMBER IN ORDER OF BIRTH | (To be answered in event of plural births) | PREMATURE / FULL TERM Yes | LEGITIMATE? Yes | DATE OF BIRTH Aug. 5th 19 26 (MONTH) (DAY) (YEAR)

FATHER

FULL NAME Jamie Richard Doe

RESIDENCE (USUAL PLACE OF ABODE) Parowan, Utah

COLOR OR RACE White AGE AT LAST BIRTHDAY 24 (YEARS)

BIRTHPLACE (CITY OR PLACE) Eagle Mountain (STATE OR COUNTRY) Utah

OCCUPATION TRADE, PROFESSION, OR PARTICULAR KIND OF WORK DONE, AS SPINNER, SAWYER, BOOKKEEPER, ETC. Writer

INDUSTRY OR BUSINESS IN WHICH WORK WAS DONE, AS SILK MILL, SAWMILL, BANK, ETC.

MOTHER

FULL MAIDEN NAME Jane Smith

RESIDENCE (USUAL PLACE OF ABODE) Parowan, Utah

COLOR OR RACE White AGE AT LAST BIRTHDAY 22 (YEARS)

BIRTHPLACE (CITY OR PLACE) Birmingham (STATE OR COUNTRY) Great Britain

OCCUPATION TRADE, PROFESSION, OR PARTICULAR KIND OF WORK DONE, AS HOUSEKEEPER, TYPIST, NURSE, CLERK, ETC. Typist

INDUSTRY OR BUSINESS IN WHICH WORK WAS DONE, AS OWN HOME, LAWYER'S OFFICE, SILK MILL, ETC. Publishing

NUMBER OF CHILDREN OF THIS MOTHER (AT TIME OF THIS BIRTH AND INCLUDING THIS CHILD) (A) BORN ALIVE AND NOW LIVING 1 (B) BORN ALIVE BUT NOW DEAD - (C) STILLBORN -

CERTIFICATE OF ATTENDING PHYSICIAN OR MIDWIFE*

I HEREBY CERTIFY THAT I ATTENDED THE BIRTH OF THIS CHILD WHO WAS Born Alive (Born alive or stillborn) AT 3:50A.M. ON THE DATE ABOVE STATED.

*When there was no attending physician or midwife, then the father, householder, etc., should make this return. A stillborn child is one that neither breathes nor shows other evidence of life after birth.

(SIGNATURE) A. J. Khan

DATE Aug 4th 19 22 M. D. (PHYSICIAN OR MIDWIFE)

ADDRESS OF PHYSICIAN OR MIDWIFE Cedar City, Utah

GIVEN NAME ADDED FROM SUPPLEMENTAL REPORT 19

FILED Aug 10th 19 22 H. J. Smith REGISTRAR

PDF files are often used when a company sends you an electronic version of a document, because they can be opened on any computer with Acrobat Reader installed—whether they were created on a Windows PC (top left) or a Mac (bottom left). PDFs can be stored in the personal records database for easy reference.

JPEG

Pronounced "jay-peg," a JPEG file is the most commonly used file format for digital images, and it has also become the almost universal default option of digital cameras. JPEG stands for Joint Photographic Experts Group (the name of the group that created it), so unsurprisingly, these files are best suited to photographs rather than fine graphics. JPEG files use a data-compression method to reduce the overall file size, so your pictures will only take up a small amount of space on your computer's hard drive. However, the compression used is known as "lossy" compression, so while it makes file sizes smaller, it also eliminates a certain amount of image detail.

Fine-quality JPEG

Compression

To control the amount of image detail that is discarded, you can specify the amount of compression in the JPEG format—either in an image-editing program, or your digital camera. Most digital cameras offer various quality settings for JPEG files, such as fine, normal, and low. If you choose the finest setting, you probably won't see any difference between a JPEG and an uncompressed file. But at the lowest JPEG setting, you may notice strange patterns called artifacts appearing around sharp edges, and textured areas may begin to lose some detail.

JPEG files are fully compatible with the database on the disc, and for the photographs you want to include, it's a good idea to choose a medium to high quality JPEG setting for good-quality images. You can also save documents as JPEG files, but if the compression setting is high—to provide a low-quality image—text can become hard to read or even illegible.

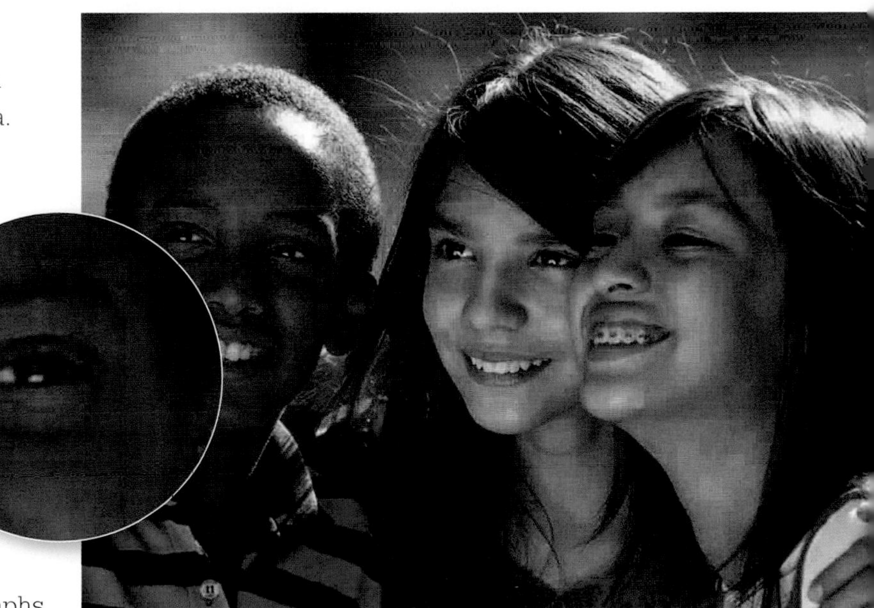

Low-quality JPEG

In the fine image, it's difficult to pinpoint any visible flaws, but if you enlarge areas of the low image, numerous artifacts become very apparent, especially around areas of fine detail.

DATABASE ESSENTIALS

Before you begin using the *Organize Your Life* program, it's important to understand a few technical basics, such as the system requirements for your computer and how to install it on a Windows PC or Apple Macintosh. This chapter covers both of these things, as well as how to open the program once you have installed it and how it operates. You will learn how to add new records, navigate, add and view images, and so on.

Since you will be compiling so much vital personal information, you will want to back up all your records to a safe place. You will discover various options, and the advantages and disadvantages of each—whether you want to store your database on a disc or print out your records for easy reference. The following pages also cover issues regarding the security of your database—with information as confidential as this you can never be too careful!

System Requirements

Running *Organize Your Life* doesn't require a very sophisticated computer setup, and all recent Microsoft Windows PC or Apple Macintosh computers will meet the minimum system requirements you need to run the program.

To start, it's important that you have enough space on your hard drive to store a copy of the database. This will let you install the program onto your computer and from that point on you can access it on your hard drive, with no need to return to the original CD.

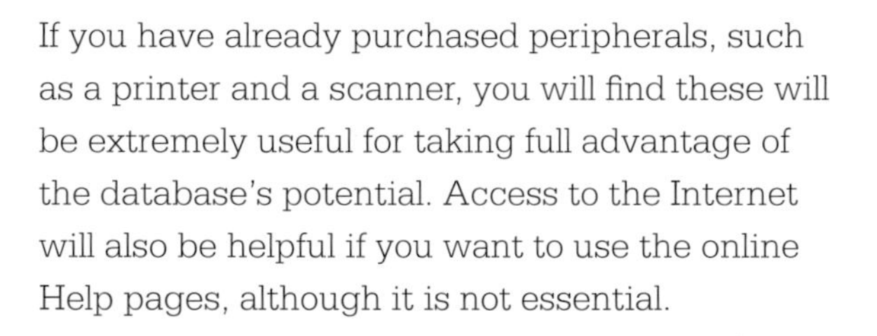

If you have already purchased peripherals, such as a printer and a scanner, you will find these will be extremely useful for taking full advantage of the database's potential. Access to the Internet will also be helpful if you want to use the online Help pages, although it is not essential.

Minimum Requirements: Windows PC

- Microsoft Windows XP, Vista, or Windows 7
- Processor (CPU): 1 GHz or faster
- Memory (RAM): 256 MB or more
- Hard-drive space: 100 MB minimum (more if you add a large number of pictures or documents)
- CD-ROM drive

Minimum Requirements: Mac OS X

- Mac OS X 10.4 or higher
- Processor (CPU): 1 GHz or faster
- Memory (RAM): 256 MB or more
- Hard-drive space: 100 MB minimum (more if you add a large number of pictures or documents)
- CD-ROM drive (for MacBook Air, access to a CD-ROM drive on another computer)

RAM is your computer's memory. This is one of the cheapest components to upgrade, and in most computers it's very easy to do this yourself.

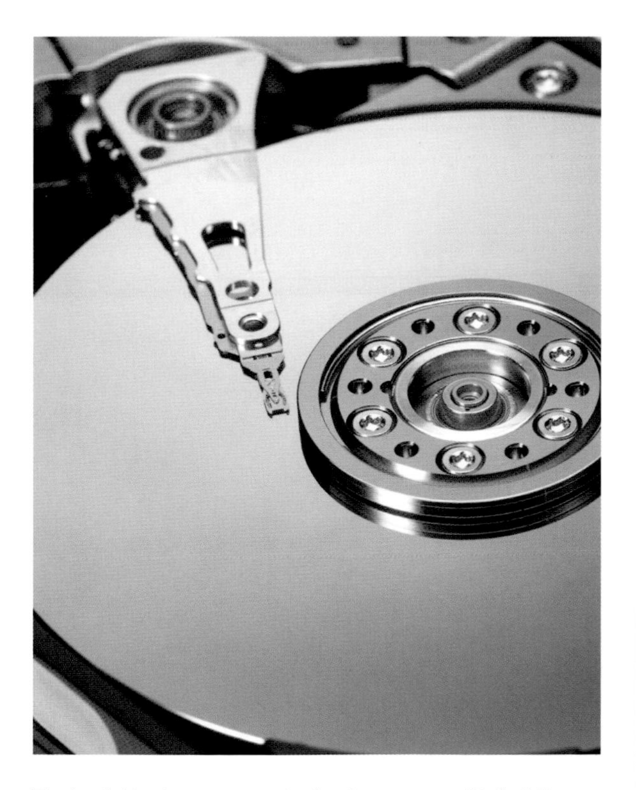

The hard drive in your computer is where you need to install *Organize Your Life*. In addition to having enough space for the program, you also need to make sure you have a minimum of 100 MB extra storage for all the documents and photos you might want to add.

Essential computer terminology

- **CPU:** The Central Processing Unit, or CPU, is your computer's "brain," and it is this part of the computer that is behind everything else that happens. The speed of the CPU is measured in Gigahertz (GHz), and the faster the processor, the quicker it can process information. To run *Organize Your Life*, the required CPU speed is very modest by modern standards.

- **RAM:** Random Access Memory (more commonly referred to as RAM) is where the computer temporarily stores information that is about to be processed by the CPU, as well as things it will need to access frequently. Generally, this means the more RAM you have in your computer, the faster it will operate. Most modern computers come with at least 1 GB (Gigabyte) of RAM, which is more than enough to run a database. But if you want to have more programs open at the same time, upgrading the RAM is often beneficial.

- **Screen Resolution:** The resolution of your computer screen refers to how much information it can display. This is measured in pixels, and the higher the number of pixels the monitor can display, the greater its resolution. For this program a minimum resolution of 1,024 x 800 pixels is recommended. This isn't particularly high, and most new computer screens will have a much higher resolution.

Installing on a Windows PC

Whether you use an Apple Macintosh (Mac) or a Windows-based personal computer (PC), the *Organize Your Life* database will look and function in the same way. However, the installation process will differ somewhat depending on which computer operating system you have chosen to use.

The CD that accompanies this book contains the program for both Windows and Macintosh operating systems. In this section, you will learn how to install the program on a PC. For Mac installation, see page 32.

While it is stored on the CD, the database cannot be altered in any way, so you need to install it on your own computer. Once the program is copied to your hard drive, you may begin adding information, documents, and photos. The installation process on a PC is kept very simple by using the automatic installer program on the disc provided. The process works as follows:

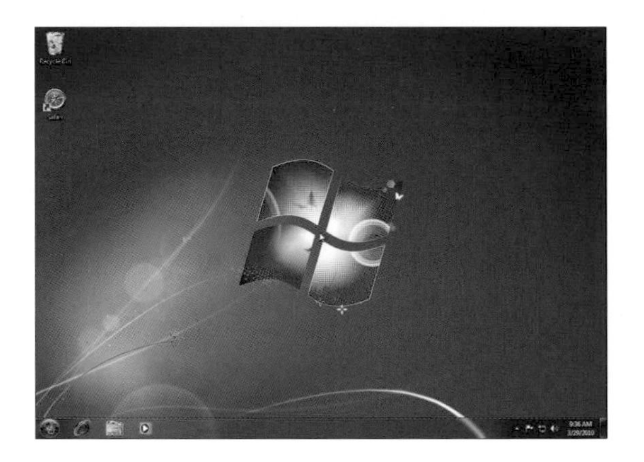

1 When you turn on your computer, log on as usual. If you already have other programs open, it's not necessary to close them as long as the Windows taskbar is visible.

User Account Control

Do you want to allow the following program from an unknown publisher to make changes to this computer?

Program name: Setup.exe
Publisher: **Unknown**
File origin: CD/DVD drive

Show details — Yes — No

Change when these notifications appear

2 To launch the installer, insert the disc into your computer's CD-ROM drive—or DVD or Blu-ray drive. After a short pause, you will automatically be offered the opportunity to run the program Setup.exe from the disc. Click *Yes* in the following dialog box to allow the installer program to make changes to your computer.

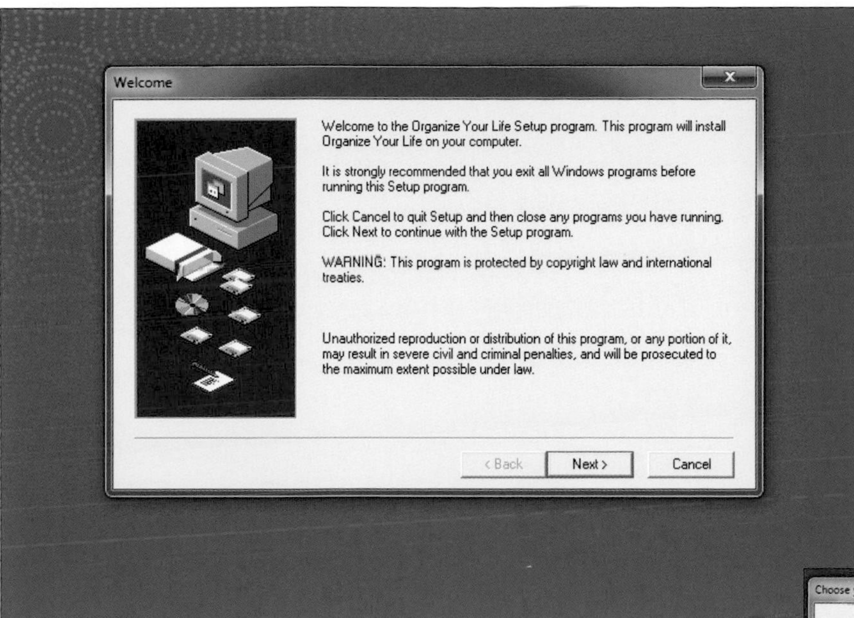

tip:

Autoplay Problems

The disc will not start automatically if you have disabled the *AutoPlay* feature on your computer. To correct this, locate the CD-ROM via Windows Explorer, right-click on it, and select *Run* from the *AutoPlay* options.

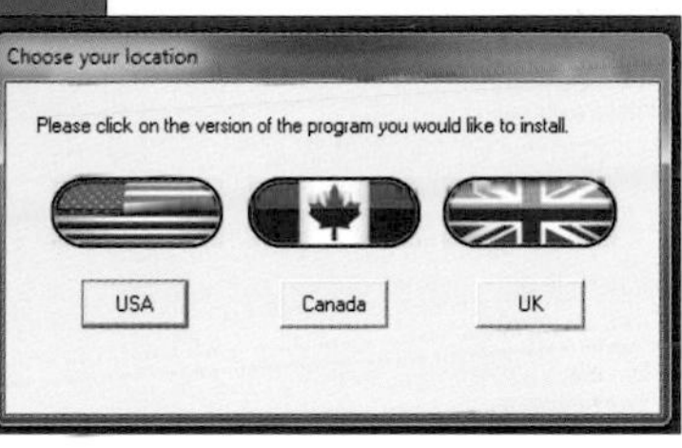

3 The installer program will now guide you through a series of steps with pages like the one above. In most cases, simply click the *Next* button.

4 You will be asked whether you live in the United States, Canada, or the United Kingdom. This affects some of the details in the database, such as the format of dates, so be sure to choose the correct country.

5 Toward the end of the installation, the installer program will place a window on the screen to show you what it has installed. You can simply close this window, because you will now be able to find the *Organize Your Life* program from the *Start* button on the taskbar because a shortcut was created.

Installing on an Apple Macintosh

The *Organize Your Life* program functions identically on a Windows-based PC or an Apple Macintosh (Mac)—it is only the installation process that differs. Here you'll learn the steps for installing the database on an Apple computer.

As previously mentioned, installing the program on your computer—whether it is a Mac or PC—is crucial, because it cannot be altered from its original form on the CD-ROM (in other words, it will not save your personal records). To function properly, it must be stored on a hard drive, such as the one built into your computer.

1 First insert the CD into the disc drive of your computer. Depending on the Mac model you are using, you may need to hold down the *Eject* button on the keyboard—rather than just tapping it—to open the CD tray.

2 There are three different versions of the database on the disc, with variations such as date format and other changes to suit the different rules and documentation in your country. Double-click on the folder for your country to be taken to the correct installer.

3 An icon will appear on your computer's desktop within a few moments. When you double-click on it, a new *Finder* window will appear with the license agreement and the *Organize Your Life* program.

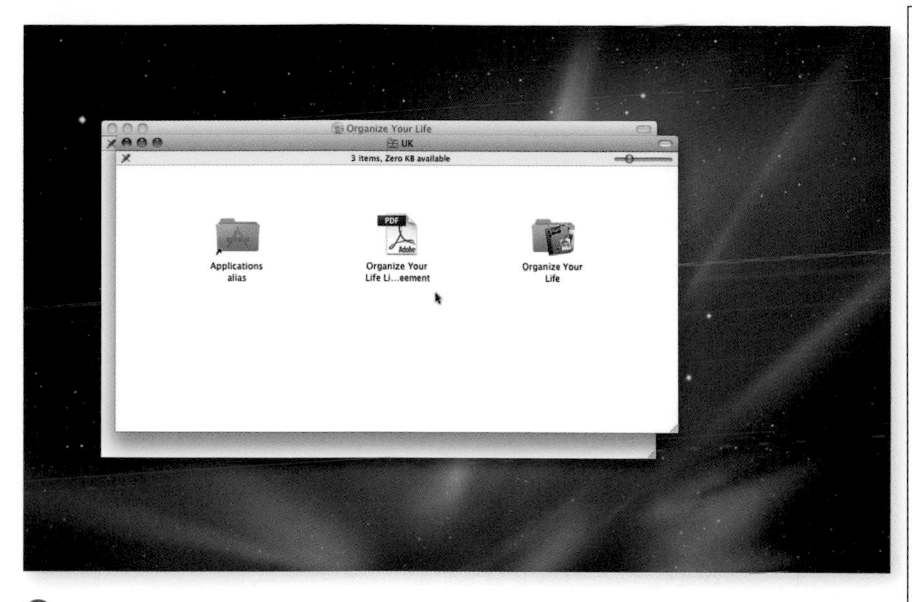

4 When the installer window opens, double click on the "Organize Your Life License Agreement" PDF file (note that the name may appear truncated on screen) and read it to make sure you agree with the program license.

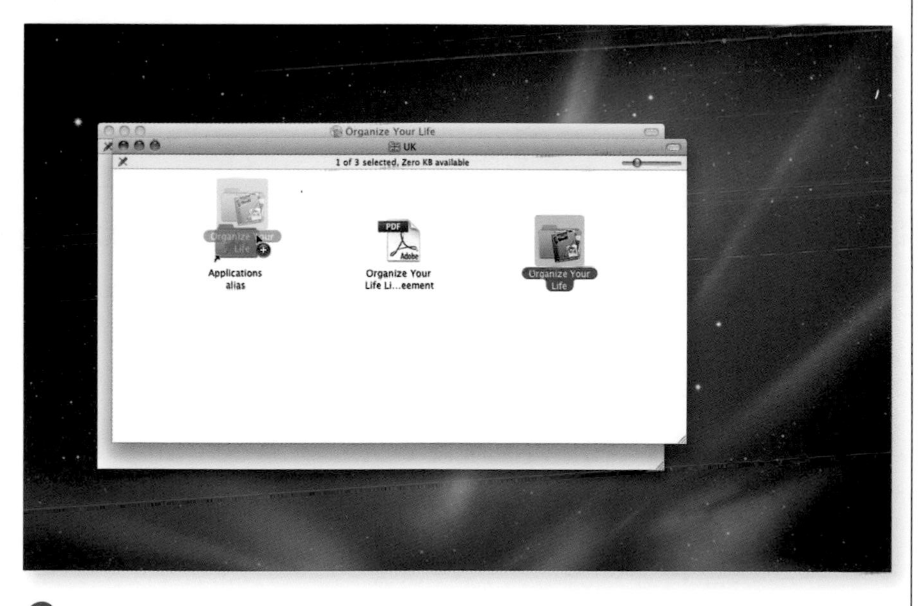

5 If you want to install the *Organize Your Life* program in the main *Applications* folder of your computer, drag its icon onto the *Applications* icon in the same folder. If you prefer to install it in an alternate location on your computer or on an external hard drive, drag the *Organize Your Life* icon to the appropriate folder or disc.

tip:

Macbook Air

There are some Apple computer models, such as the super-thin MacBook Air, which come without a CD-ROM drive to reduce their size and weight. If your computer does not have a CD-ROM drive, you will still be able to install the program, but you will need access to either a computer that does include a CD-ROM drive or to an external drive.

For installation using an external drive, just connect it to your computer and follow the instructions provided. To install the program using another computer, install the remote disc software on that computer, and then read the disc by selecting the *Remote Disc* option from the *Finder* window's sidebar (the column of icons shown at left).

Opening the Database

Once you've installed *Organize Your Life,* the program will be stored with all your other programs, and it is very easy to access from the computer's *Start* menu (Windows) or *Applications* folder (Mac).

If you chose to add a desktop shortcut during the installation process, you will see an icon for the database on your desktop. This is not the actual program, just a link to it that you can double-click to launch the program.

Desktop alias

Removing desktop shortcuts

The database's icon has a white box with a curving arrow in the lower-left corner; this indicates that the file on the desktop is a shortcut. This means that you can safely delete the shortcut if you find your desktop is becoming too cluttered with programs, and you won't delete the program itself. To delete the shortcut from your desktop, simply drag the icon to the Recycle Bin.

After you have installed *Organize Your Life,* it will be highlighted in the *Start* menu to make it easier to find. On subsequent occasions you may need to click the *All Programs* button to locate it, or type "Organize Your Life" into the *Start* menu's search box.

Creating a taskbar shortcut (Windows 7)

To make your database easy to access on your PC, you can keep it on the taskbar at the bottom of the screen so you can launch the program with a single click. To add the program to the taskbar, open the database from the *Start* menu and right click on its icon on the taskbar. Choose *Pin this program to taskbar* from the menu.

Opening on a Mac

On a Mac, programs can be stored anywhere on your computer, but it makes sense to keep them in the *Applications* folder. That's where *Organize Your Life* will be if you followed the standard installer instructions.

1 To launch the database, open the *Applications* folder on your computer and locate the *Organize Your Life* folder.

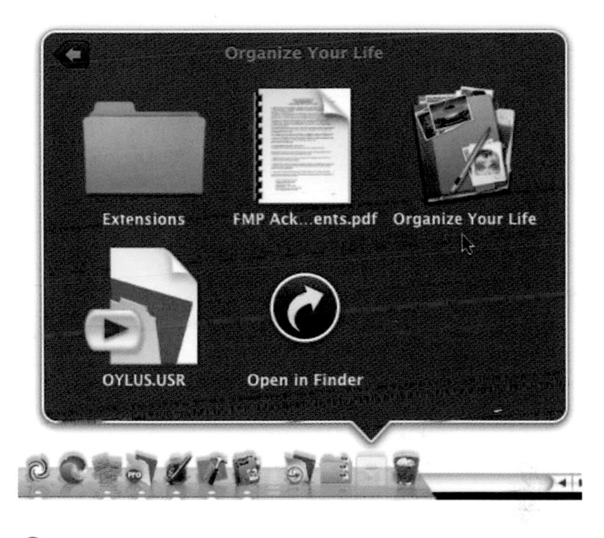

2 Open the *Organize Your Life* folder, then select and double-click the *Organize Your Life* program to launch it.

3 To create a permanent shortcut to the program on the Dock at the bottom of your desktop, press and hold the Ctrl key and click on the *Organize Your Life* icon. Choose *Keep in Dock* from the *Options* menu.

Security

You will be using *Organize Your Life* to store a lot of your personal information, and not all of it will be something you want other people to see. To keep your data safe, the program is password protected, which means only someone who knows your password can access your records.

1 When you start the *Organize Your Life* program for the first time, a dialog box will automatically open that asks you to set your password. For your security, you need to set a password before you can access the database.

Set Password

Use these fields to set the password for Organize Your Life. Please enter your new password twice.

New Password:

Confirm New Password:

Password Hint:

Cancel OK

Set Password

Use these fields to set the password for Organize Your Life. Please enter your new password twice.

New Password:

••••••••

Confirm New Password:

••••••••

Password Hint:

first dog's name

Cancel OK

Enter your chosen password in the *New Password* field at the center of the dialog box. The letters and numbers you use for your password won't be shown as you type, so no one can see what you are entering

Enter your password a second time in the *Confirm New Password* field. Be careful to enter the password correctly.

Finally, add a *Password Hint*. This should be something that will remind you what your password is, but should NOT be the password itself.

Once you have entered your password, confirmed it, and set a *Password Hint,* press *OK* to move on. If the information you have entered in the new password fields matches, you will see a window confirming the password has been set. If not, you will be asked to set your password again.

Set Password

Your password has been successfully set

OK

2 Whenever you open *Organize Your Life* and click on one of the nine subjects, you will be asked to enter your password. Once you have done this successfully you can navigate freely through the sections, as described on pages 38–41.

However, there is one exception to this. Every time you want to access the Safe Place section—whether it is from the opening page or by using the navigation tabs in the program—you will be asked to resupply your password. This is to make sure that if you are away from your computer and have left the records program open, no one has access to your most-important information.

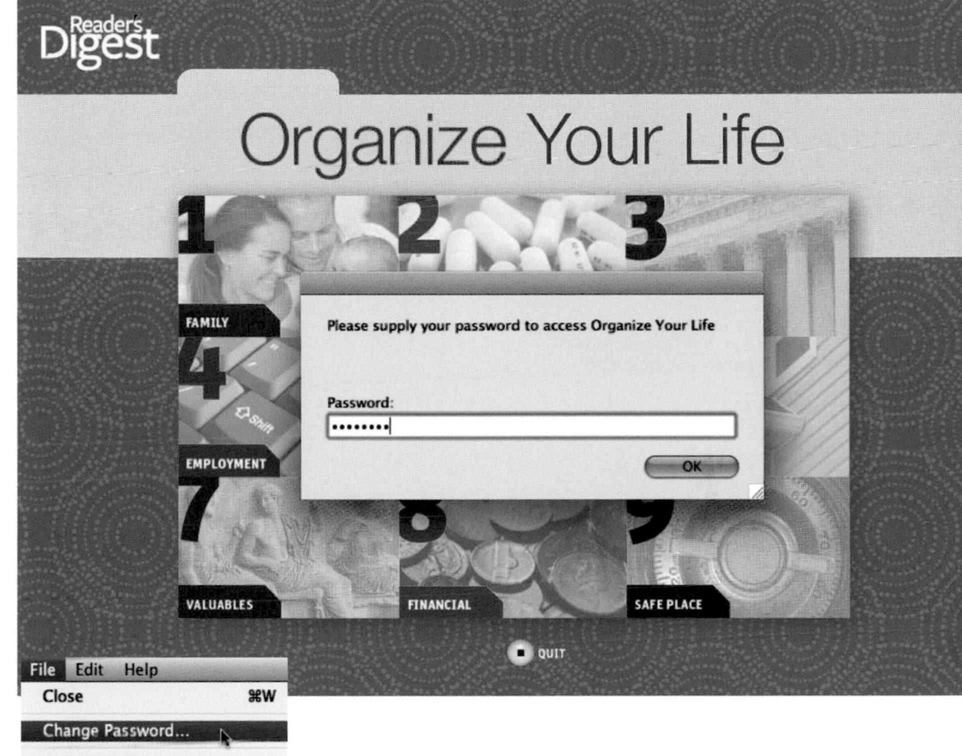

Page Setup...

Change Password

Use these fields to change the password for your Home Organiser. Please enter your old password once and your new password twice.

Old Password:

New Password:

Confirm New Password:

Cancel OK

Change Hint

Your password has been successfully changed. Use the field below to change your password hint

Password Hint:

name of first school

OK

3 You can change your password at any time by choosing *File>Change Password* from the Main Menu bar at the top of the screen.

In the *Change Password* dialog box there are three fields to fill in: *Old Password, New Password,* and *Confirm New Password*. None of these will show the keystrokes you make, so be sure to enter the information carefully. Start by entering your current (old) password, then the one you would like to change it to. Enter the new password again to confirm it, then press *OK*.

If the information you entered is OK, a dialog box will open to confirm your password has been changed successfully. The dialog also contains a field that allows you to update your password hint. When you have done this, click *OK*. You have now changed your password.

Navigation

Once you have opened *Organize Your Life* and set your password, you are ready to start creating and adding your records. But first it's worth taking a tour of the program so you know how to navigate your way around it to get the best from its many features.

Navigating within the database is very straightforward. When you first open the program, you will be presented with an opening screen that lets you choose any one of the nine categories to view or edit.

Alternatively, all the available topics are always visible at the top of your screen, no matter what page you are on, so at any time you can click on one of these tabs to switch to a different section: The section you are currently working in will be highlighted.

The only category that you cannot enter automatically is the Safe Place, which will require you to enter your password.

When you open *Organize Your Life,* you will be presented with the opening screen. From here you can choose any one of the nine available categories to view or edit.

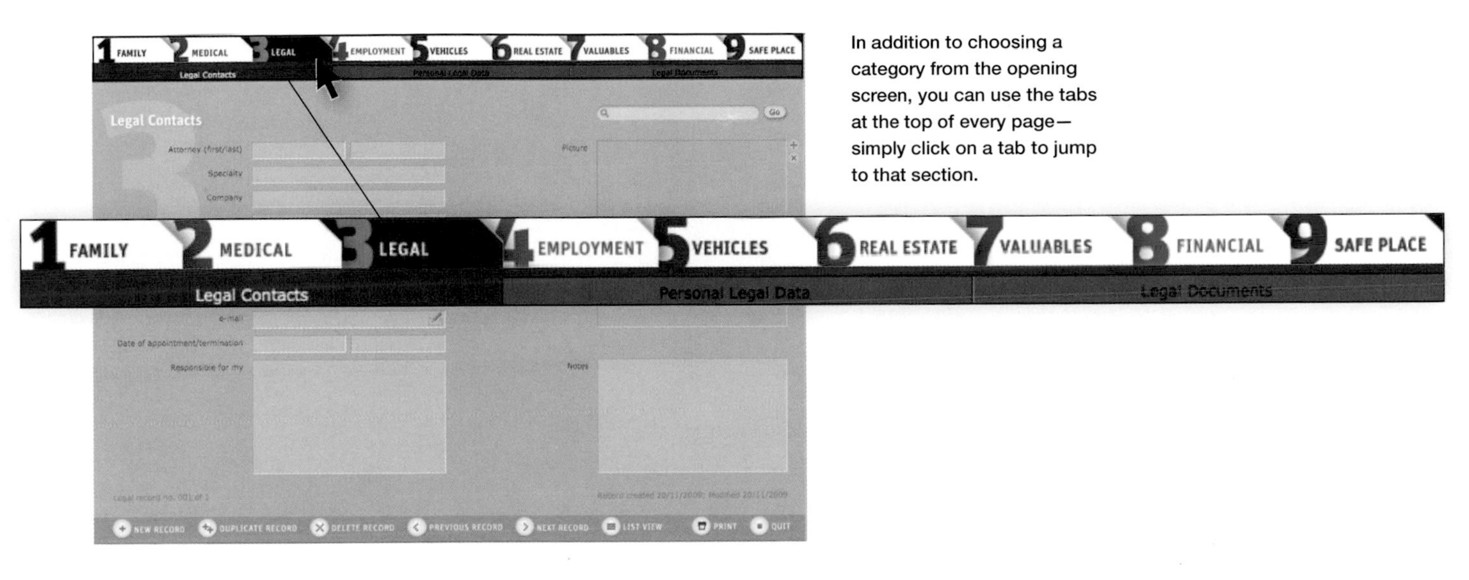

In addition to choosing a category from the opening screen, you can use the tabs at the top of every page—simply click on a tab to jump to that section.

Below the category tabs you will find links to all the records available within that category. In some categories the number of options can be extensive, while other categories may have only a single record available.

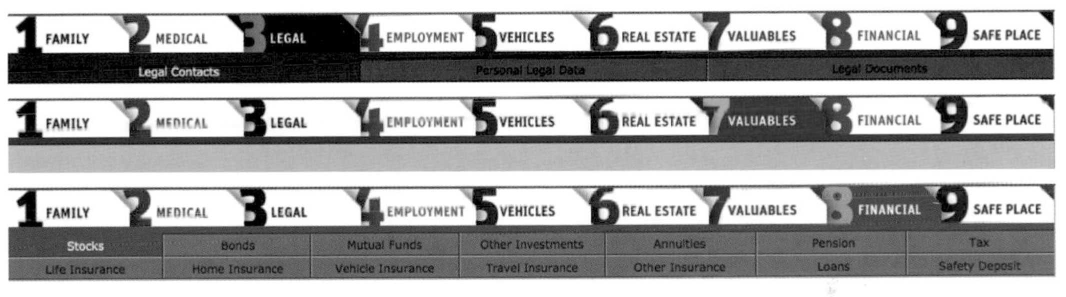

Icons explained

As you add your records and fill in the database, you will notice three different icons that appear throughout the program.

Autofill

Clicking on this icon will automatically insert the information you have entered in your Personal Data, such as your name or address.

E-mail

When you click on the E-mail icon, which appears in all E-mail fields in the database, your e-mail program will open with a new, blank e-mail.

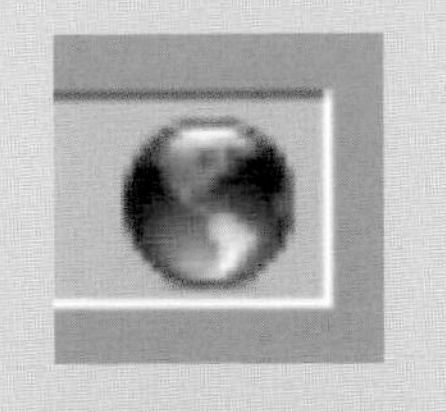

Web

Located in fields with website addresses, the Web icon will open up your Internet browser and take you directly to the specified webpage.

→

Record screens

All the categories are set up with single or multiple records screens. You will be able to distinguish between the two immediately, because single record screens only display the *Print* and *Quit* buttons. Multiple records screens include a longer list of options along the bottom, as described below.

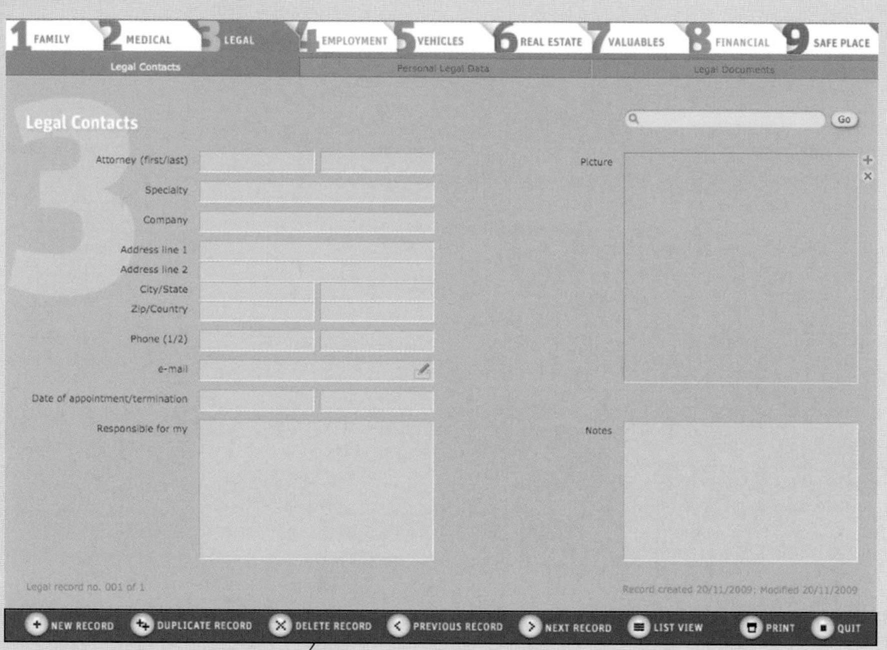

NEW RECORD DUPLICATE RECORD DELETE RECORD PREVIOUS RECORD NEXT RECORD LIST VIEW PRINT QUIT

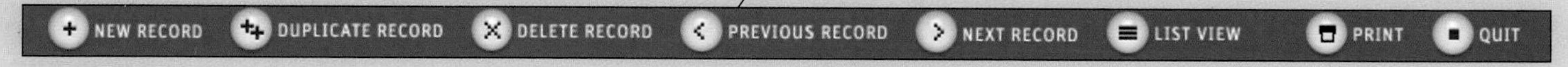

New Record

Creates an additional record.

Duplicate Record

Creates an exact duplicate of the current record, which you can then edit.

Delete Record

Completely eliminates the record you have on the screen from the database.

Previous Record and Next Record

View other records you have already created.

List View

Allows you to see all your records for one screen's subject listed at a glance.

Print

Enables you to print out the open database page (or list view). See pages 60–61 for more details on printing.

Quit

Closes the *Organize Your Life* program.

List View

The *List View* format dedicates one line to each record in a particular category. This displays less information than is offered on the full record screen, but it is the most essential data, and it allows you to see all the records in a specific category at a glance.

Clicking on any of the column headers will sort the list into alphabetical or numerical order based on that column's content. This allows you to sort your records by name or date, for example, instead of displaying them by record number.

To return to the full record for any subject, select the appropriate record by scrolling up and down the screen with the arrows on your keyboard or by clicking the *Previous Record* and *Next Record* buttons. When you have located the record you want to view in full, click the *Full Record* button at the bottom of the screen and *Organize Your Life* will open the record on-screen for you to view or edit.

Drop-down menus

A navigational feature that appears in a number of fields throughout the database is a drop-down menu. To notify you that a field contains a drop-down menu, a downward pointing arrow will appear when you click on the field.

When you click on the arrow, a list of options will be displayed. If you would like to add something to the drop-down list that isn't already there, choose *Edit* from the menu. This will let you edit the drop-down options, so you can add or delete an existing one to personalize the program, so it only includes the options you need.

Record	Manufacturer	Model	License plate	Year	Date purchased	Cost	Date sold	Price
001	Ford	Model T		1928	03/04/1929	$312.00	05/06/1937	$136.00
002	Chevrolet	Corvette	VBK-7838		12/03/2010	$48,930.00		
003	GMC	Sierra XFE	ENB-2316	2010	02/01/2010	$32,000.00		
004	Ford	Mustang	SKJ-6548	1966	03/04/2006	$16,000.00	12/03/2010	$18,[illegible]
005	Austin	Princess	AGC 138K	1956	05/09/1972	$500.00	11/11/1985	$10[illegible]
008	Toyota	Prius	AB-1234	2006	07/12/2008	$13,600.00	04/01/2008	$9.8[illegible]

FULL RECORD

The *List View* shows you all the records in a particular category at a glance. You can use the *Full Record* button to display the record in full.

Creating a New Record

The first step in the process of filling in your records is to decide which category you want to add information to: Family, Medical, Legal, and so on. You can choose the category from the start screen or by using the tabs at the top of each page.

Once you have chosen the category, such as medical, you can navigate to the relevant subcategory, such as Medical Contacts, Personal Medical Profile, or Personal Medical Record.

1 Choose a category from the opening screen or the tabs at the top of every page...

2 ...and then choose your subcategory from the top menu.

Saving your records

As you enter your records, you obviously want to make sure that the information isn't lost if your computer crashes unexpectedly. However, you don't need to remember to save your records at frequent intervals or even save any changes you have made before you quit the program—everything you add to the database is saved automatically as you enter it.

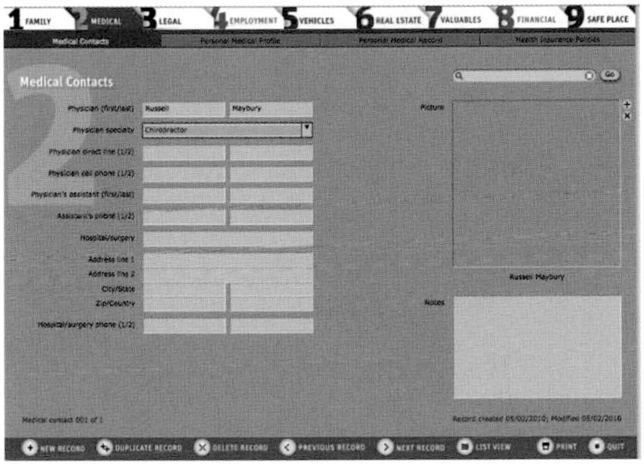

3 Each new page of information you create is a new record, and the database provides a blank record for every category to get you started. Some areas can be covered by a single record—such as your personal medical record or your current employment—while other sections might need multiple records: family members, physicians, vehicles, or residences, for example. To enter the information, simply click on an empty field box and type.

4 If you need to create a new record for the same subject—to add a new Medical Contact, for example—click on the *New Record* button at the bottom of the screen once you have completed the first record. This will create a new, blank record for you to fill in. Alternatively, if there will be a lot of information that is common to both records, you can use the *Duplicate Record* button. This saves you from retyping everything: You can simply change any fields that are different by entering the new information in the field.

Adding and Viewing Images

Many of the records in the database allow you to add images and documents. If you have an image you would like to add, it needs to be in JPEG format, while a document will need to be scanned and saved this way, too. Once you have your "digital document" you are ready to add it to the database.

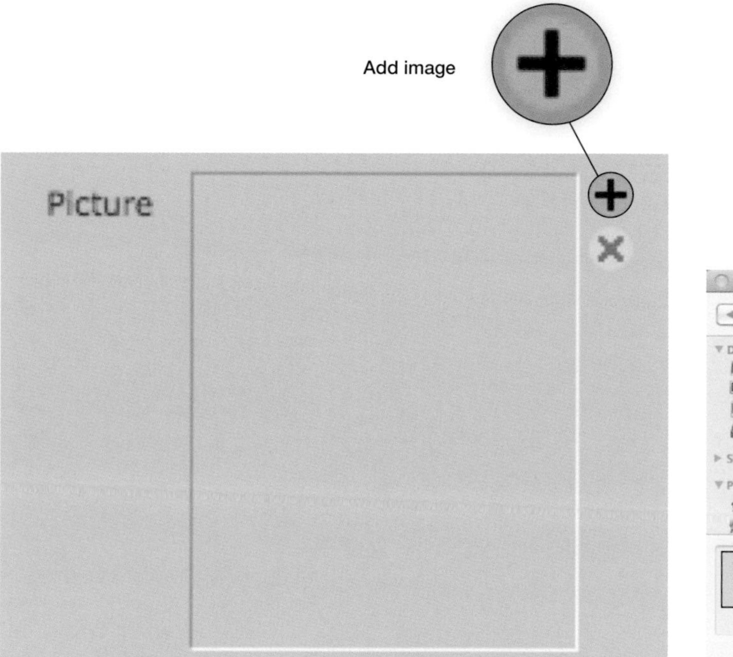

1 Fields where you may upload images and documents will be labeled Document, Picture, or Image. You will see a green + icon at the right side of the field, which is the *Add Image/ Document* icon. Click on the icon to open a dialog box that allows you to browse within your computer files to select the photo or document of your choice.

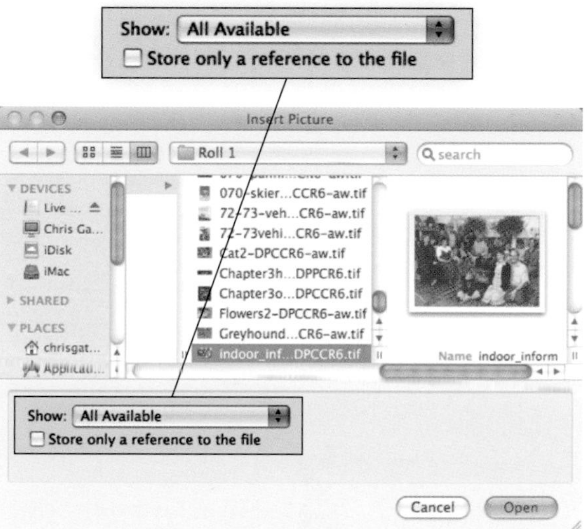

2 At the bottom of the *Insert Picture* window is the option to *Store only a reference to the file*. If this option is unchecked, the image or document will be stored within the database, although it is a good idea to keep the original file as well.

However, if this option is checked, the database will simply remember where the file is on your computer, rather than copying it into the database. This will prevent you from duplicating the file on your computer's hard drive, but it is important that you do not move the original file if you choose this option. If you do, the database will not know where to find it.

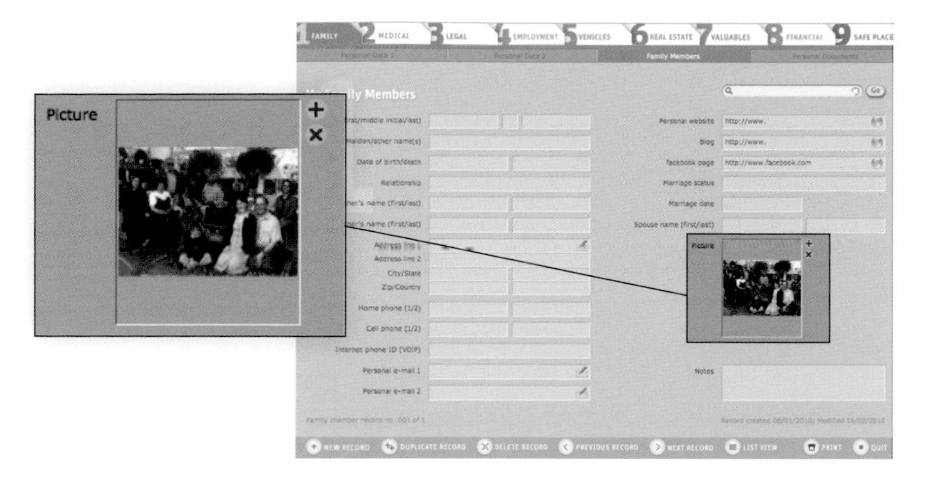

3 Once you have located the image or document you want to add, click *Open* and the file will immediately appear in the field.

Removing and replacing files

If you wish to remove (or replace) an image or document that you have already uploaded, click on the red x icon next to the picture field, and the file will be deleted from the database. You can then insert a new document or image in its place.

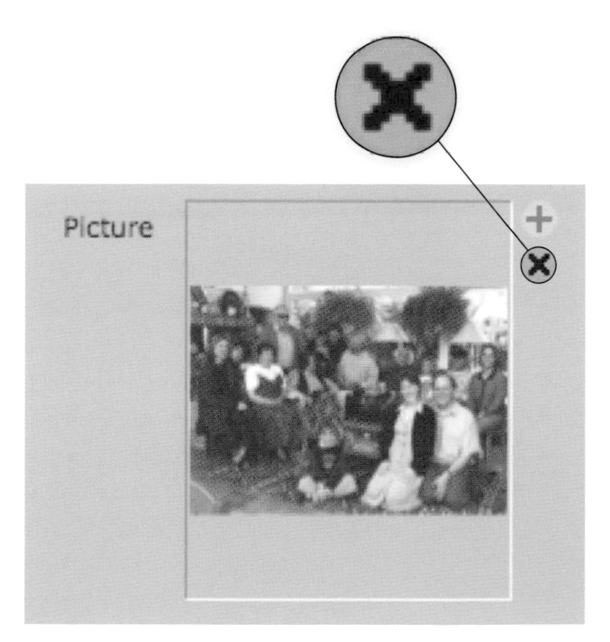

Viewing photographs and documents

To enlarge your view of a photograph or document, click on the image or document preview to open it in a new window. At the bottom of this window you will find two buttons—*Print Document* and *Close Window*.

Some companies or suppliers may provide you with electronic documentation, which is usually in the form of multipage PDF files. While you can include these in your records, it is important to note that only the first page will be visible and only the first page can be printed. (For more on printing see pages 60–61.)

Searching the Database

If you used to store all your personal records in a filing cabinet, you'll probably know what it's like when you need to find a certain piece of information: You have to try and remember which document you need and then look through all your paperwork to find it.

However, with your records stored in a database on your computer, the search and retrieval procedure becomes much easier. Instead of looking through your records yourself, you can get your computer to do all the hard work for you by using *Organize Your Life's* sophisticated *Search* feature.

Basic search

The *Search* feature appears at the top right of every page, so no matter where you are in the program or what record you're viewing, you can initiate a search.

To start a search, click on the search field and type in the term that you want. Then click on the *Go* button and the search engine will go through every field, in all of the records in the program (except for your Safe Place data), looking for records that contain text or numbers that match your search. It could be a name, a place, a date, or any other word you have used in any of your records.

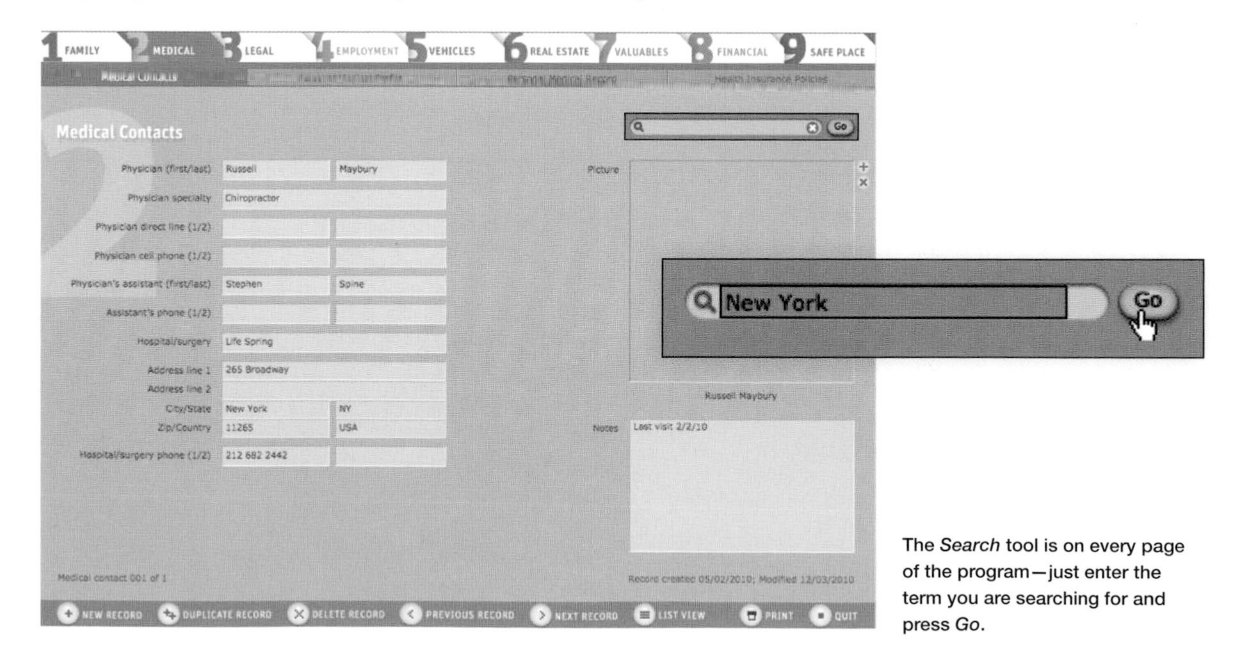

The *Search* tool is on every page of the program—just enter the term you are searching for and press *Go*.

Viewing your search results

After it trawls through your records, a new window will open that gives you the results of your search. In the *Results* window, every record containing a field that matches your search criteria will be listed. The results are listed under a heading for the database section they appear in (Personal Records, Medical, Legal, and so on), along with the number of results found and the unique record number for the match.

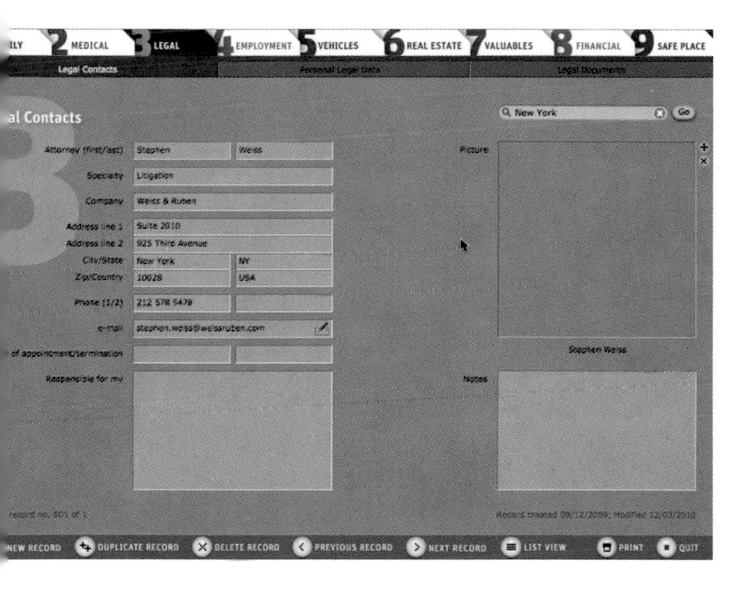

If you want to change your search criteria, you can return to the records page and enter a new search term or, with the Results window open, use the *Search* box at the top of the dialog box. Both options will initiate a new search, but if you search using the *Results* dialog box, you will have to press the *Enter* key on your keyboard or click on the *Magnifying Glass* icon, instead of pressing a *Go* button.

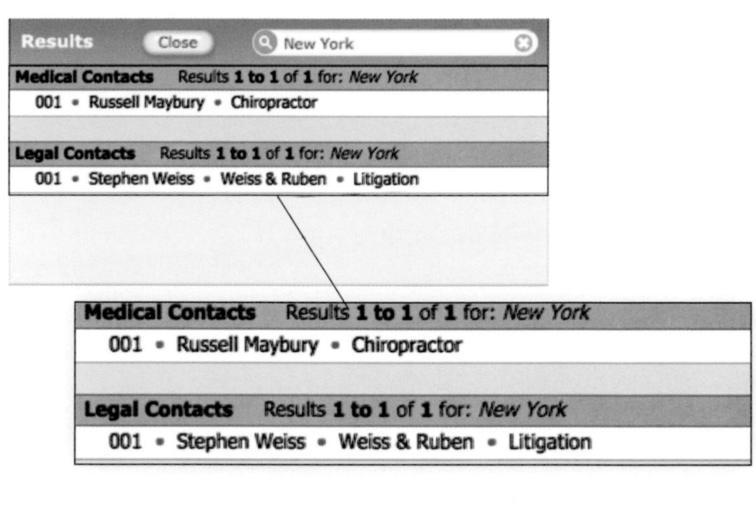

To view any of the search results, click on the record name in the *Results* window and the program will open the appropriate record. If it isn't the one you wanted, you can click on another record in the *Results* window to skip to a different page.

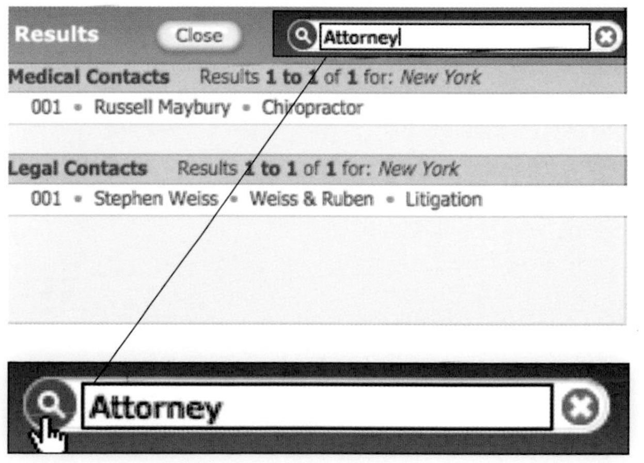

→

Searching for dates

When you are searching for a date, it's a good idea to enter the whole date where possible, using the date format that is appropriate for your region (MM/DD/YYYY in the United States or DD/MM/YYYY in Canada). So, for example, if you wanted to search for February 4, 2011, in the U.S. version of the program, you would enter 2/4/11 and the search engine would list all the records containing that specific day.

It is also possible to search for records by month or year, by substituting an asterisk into the date. For example, searching for 2/*/11 would reveal all the records dated February 2011, while entering */*/11 in the *Search* field will find all the records that include a 2011 date.

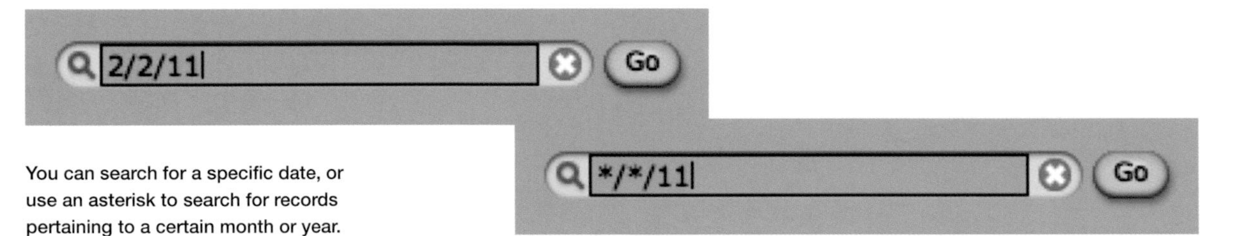

You can search for a specific date, or use an asterisk to search for records pertaining to a certain month or year.

Safe searching

The search tool looks through all the fields in every record on the program, with the exception of your Safe Place information. This is to assure that anyone who has access to your computer cannot search for your bank account details, credit card information, or anything else you want to keep secure in that section of the program.

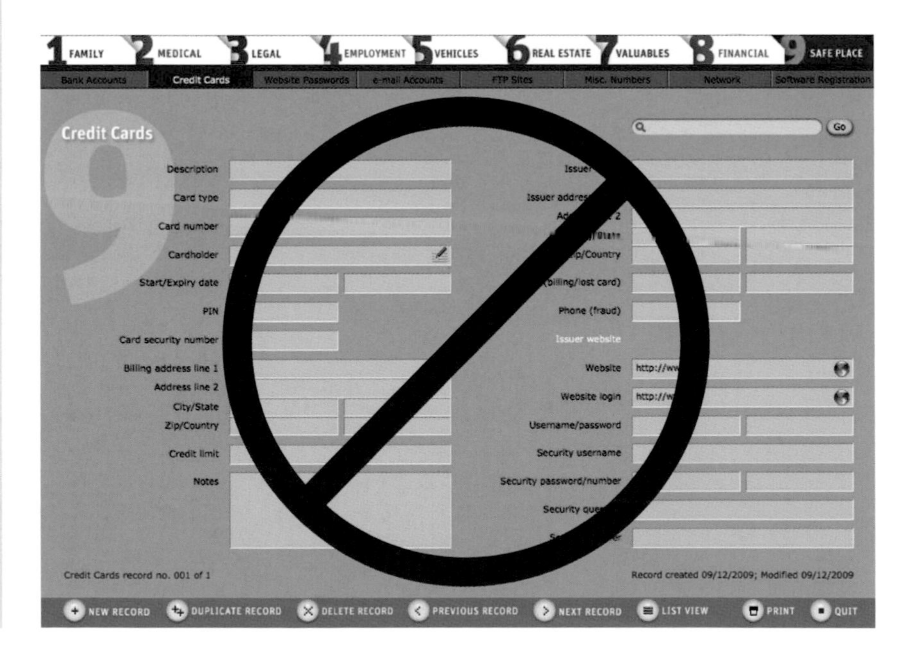

Searching shortcuts

You don't need to type in a full phrase to conduct a search—just one word will work. For example, if you were searching for addresses in New York, you could search for "New" or "York" and the program would find the relevant records.

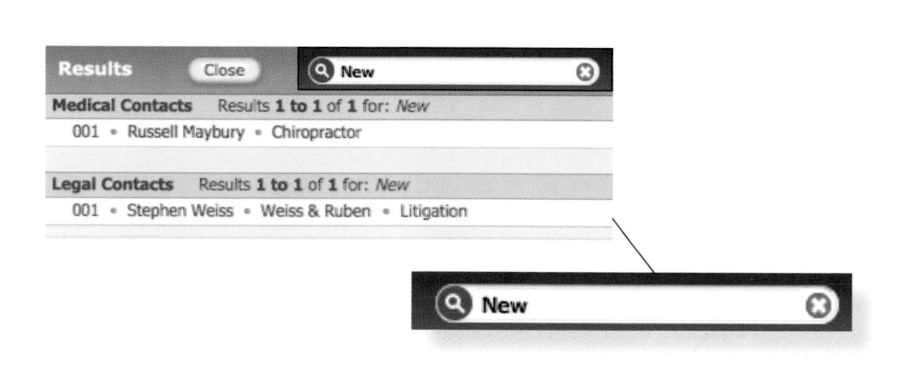

> **tip:**
> **Check your spelling**
> Although there is little more to searching the database than entering your search term and clicking *Go*, the *Search* feature is looking for an exact match to the words or numbers you enter. This means that if you have spelled something incorrectly in a record, but enter it correctly in the search box, the *Search* tool will not find it.

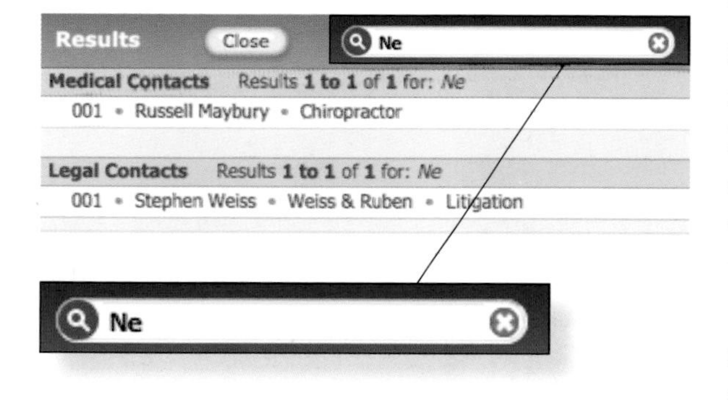

You can condense the search term even more: Searching for "Ne" or "Yo," for example, will still find all your New York entries. You must be sure your search term consists of at least two characters, and that they are at the start of the word you are looking for: Searching for "ew" or "rk" will not find entries matching New York.

Although this saves you from typing out the full word in the search box, there is a downside: the search feature will locate *all* the fields that have information starting with the same two letters, so you may end up with more results than if you entered the full word.

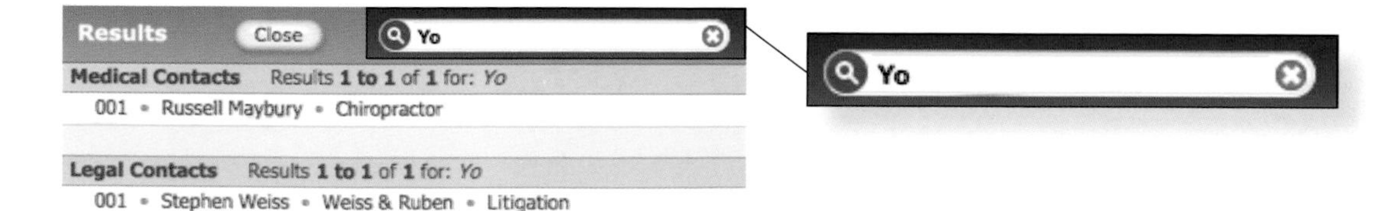

Backing Up to a Disc

Once you have invested your time finding and entering your records into the database, you'll want to keep them protected from potential damage or loss. No computer is 100 percent risk-free from failure, so be sure to make a backup copy of your records to be stored someplace else.

All computers are generally supplied with an optical media drive, whether it is a CD, DVD, or Blu-ray drive, and blank discs can be purchased at a relatively low cost. Once you've saved your record on a disc, you can keep it separate from your computer in a secure location.

The question of whether your computer is a Windows-based PC or an Apple Mac will determine how you back up to a disc. We have included instructions for both operating systems. (Note that the instructions for Windows 7 apply to Windows Vista and XP, too.)

WINDOWS 7 (PC)

1 Before you copy the database to a disc or any other media, make sure the *Organize Your Life* program is not currently in use. To quit the program, choose *Quit* from any records page.

2 Insert a blank CD or DVD into your computer's optical drive. After a few moments, your computer will recognize the disc and present a number of options. From these, select *Burn Files to Disc*.

3 You will have to name your disc before copying your records onto it. Keep the name practical and to the point, and remember you may use a maximum of 16 characters. Including an abbreviated month and year is always an option for easy recall. Beneath the name box are two options, which allow you to choose how the disc behaves. For maximum reuse of the same disc, choose the option *Like a USB flash drive*.

4 Once your disc is prepared you will be offered the option to open folders in Windows Explorer. Choose this option.

5 The whole database is kept with your computer's Program Files. To locate it, first click on the *Computer>Local Disk (:C)* option in the left sidebar. Then double-click on the *Program Files (x86)* folder.

tip:

Write once or multisession?

Depending on your preference, discs can be formatted so that data is recorded onto them either a single time for permanent storage or multiple times.

When Windows asks whether the disc should behave *Like a USB flash drive* or whether you want to use it *With a CD/DVD player*, it is determining how to write onto the disc.

Windows XP and later versions can read and write to the same disc a number of times, treating it as a reusable drive. The main difference is that if it is not a rewriteable disc, you will eventually run out of space.

When you delete or replace a file on the disc with a newer one, Windows removes the file from the list in Windows Explorer. However, the space it occupies on the disc cannot be reused.

→

6 Inside Program Files is the *Organize Your Life* folder, which contains all of the database's component parts. To back up the database, simply click on this folder and drag it to the icon for your CD in the sidebar to the left. On most computers this will be called the D: drive. Be sure not to click on any files other than those mentioned here, because this is an important directory to your computer.

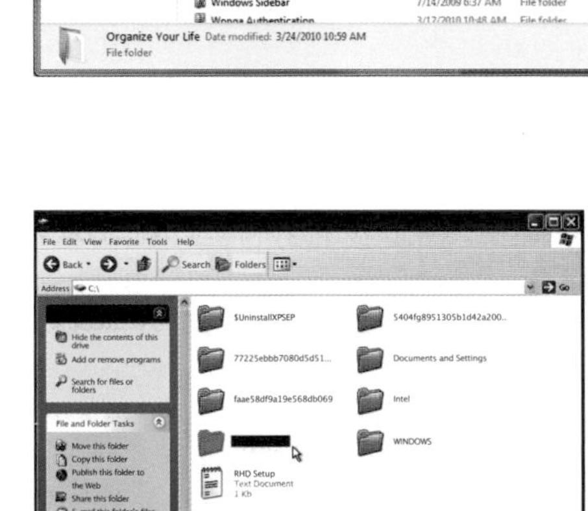

7 When all the files have been copied to the disc, right-click on the disc's icon in the Windows Explorer sidebar and choose the *Eject* option. This tells the computer you want to eject the disc and allows Windows to complete some necessary tasks. Do not simply press the eject button on your CD drive.

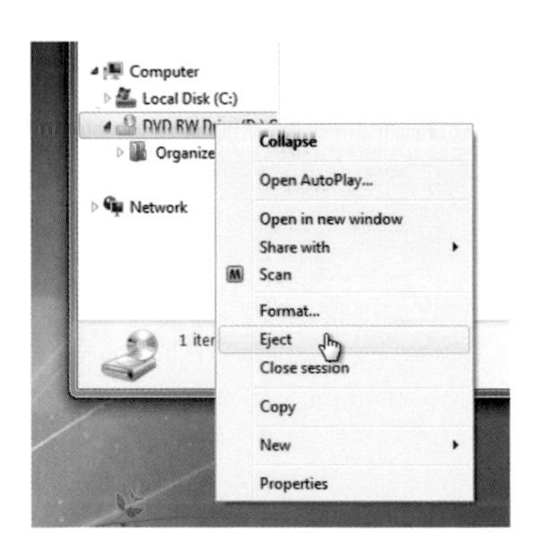

8 Close session

Before the disc is ejected, the session on the disc is closed, which means that Windows adds some data to help it find and understand the files next time you use the disc. The disc is then ejected when it's ready.

tip:

Archival media

The format of optical discs is much more durable and certainly more convenient than earlier forms of discs and tapes, but it's unlikely that something this cheap will last indefinitely. After a few years, CDs and DVDs will begin to degrade; the edges of a disc are particularly vulnerable, and when exposed to moisture, the recording layer can actually produce visible damage.

If you take care to store your discs away from moisture and direct light, good-quality, archival discs can be extremely long-lasting, remaining intact for more than 100 years. However, it is still a good idea to copy your discs' contents every few years onto new ones or simply update your archive copy of the database. Periodically copying onto new discs will also ensure that they are compatible with the most up-to-date computer models.

MAC

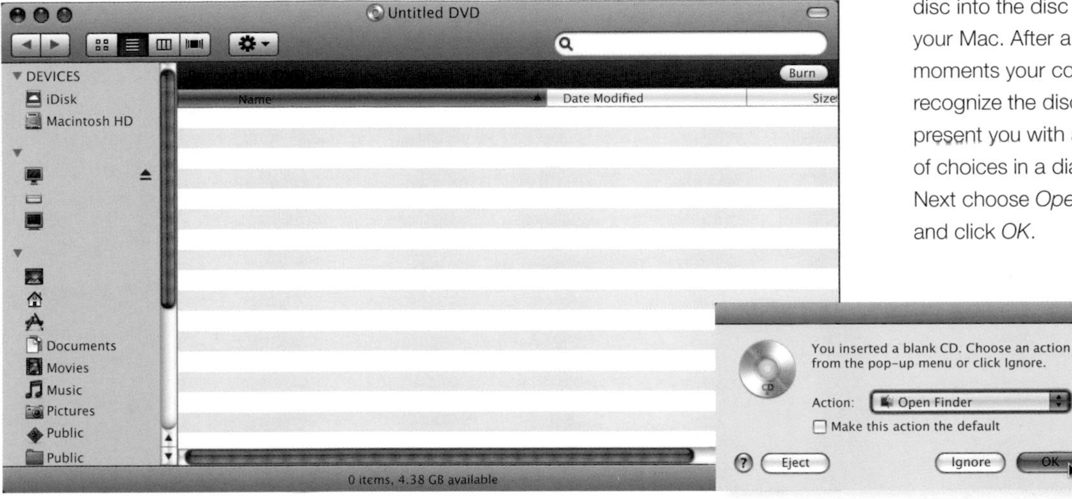

1 Quit the database program and insert a blank disc into the disc drive of your Mac. After a few moments your computer will recognize the disc and present you with a number of choices in a dialog box. Next choose *Open Finder* and click *OK*.

2 An *Untitled Disc* icon will appear on your desktop; double-click on it to open a special *Finder* window called a *Burn* folder. This functions the same as any standard folder, the only difference is that when you drag your files into it, this folder creates links to your files instead of copying or moving them. This means that the original location of your files remains unchanged.

3 Press Apple+Shift+N from the Finder to open a second *Finder* window, then select the *Applications* icon from the sidebar to view all your available programs. Locate the *Organize Your Life* folder and drag it from the *Applications* folder to the *Burn* folder.

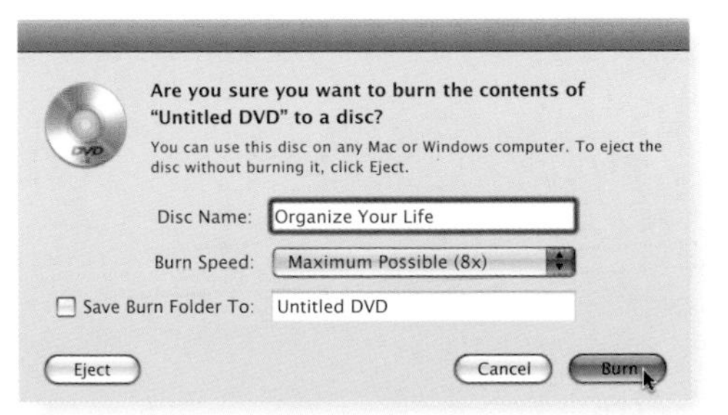

4 Press the *Burn* button located in the toolbar at the top of the folder contents. When prompted, name your disc and click *OK*. When the disc has been recorded, you can safely eject it, label it, and file your backup disc somewhere secure.

Backing Up to a USB Stick

Burning the contents of your archive to a durable optical disc is a practical way to back up your files, but it is not your only option. One extremely practical storage option is a USB stick—a flash-memory data-storage device that you plug into your computer's USB (Universal Serial Bus) port.

USB sticks are available in numerous designs and capacities. They are generally compact—so small that they often fit on a keychain—and durable enough to carry around in your pocket without worrying about potential damage. Copying your files to a USB stick is very simple and, unlike CDs or DVDs, there is no issue regarding the choice of single or multiple uses: A USB stick can have files written to it as often as you like.

1 To store files onto a USB stick, insert it into an available USB port. These are usually located on the back of your computer, but they are sometimes found on the sides, front, or even on the keyboard or monitor.

2 The computer will take a few moments to detect the USB stick. When it asks you what you want do with it, select *Open Folder to View Items*. An Explorer window will pop up.

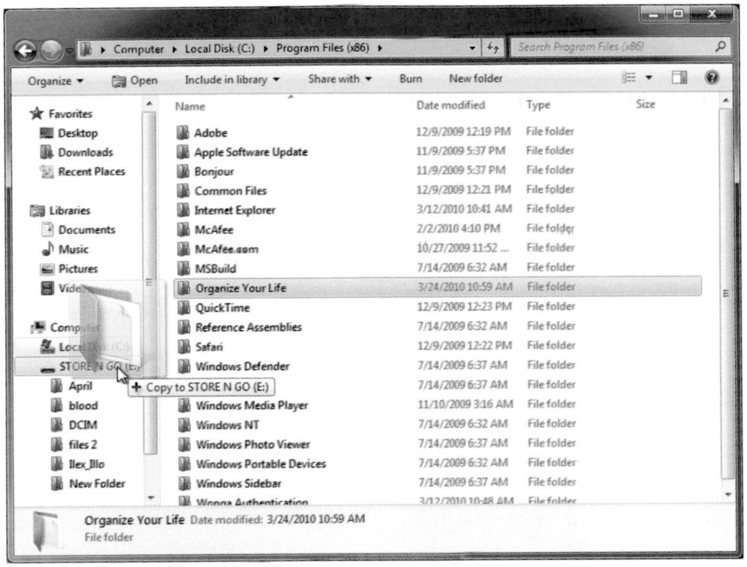

tip:

USB sticks on a Mac

Copying files onto a USB stick on a Mac is just as simple as on a PC.

Insert the stick into a USB socket, and it will show up on your desktop as an external drive.

Select the *Organize Your Life* folder in your *Applications* folder and drag it to the *USB stick* icon to copy your files.

When your files have been copied, drag the *USB stick* icon to the trash to eject it. Once the icon disappears from the desktop, you can safely remove the USB stick.

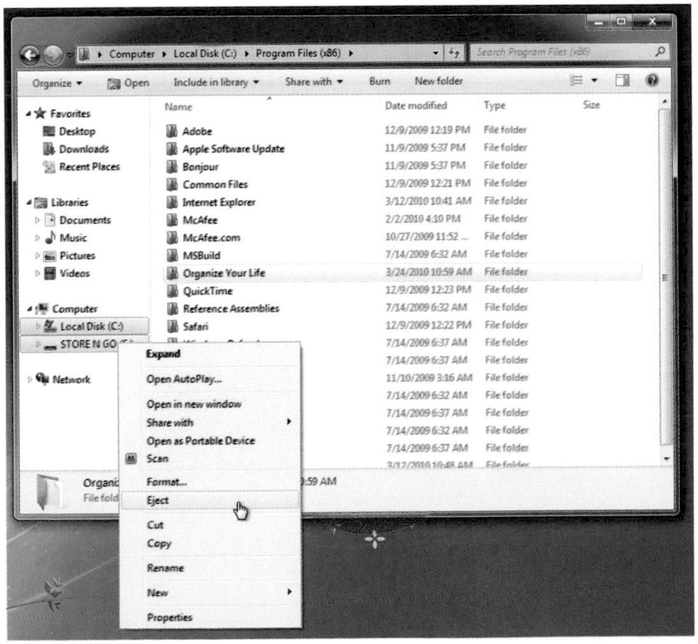

3 Click once on the C: drive (your computer's hard drive), where you should find the *Organize Your Life* folder. Drag the *Organize Your Life* folder onto the number or letter of the USB stick's drive. In the example shown above, the drive is labeled E: and named BACK_UP.

4 When all the files have been copied, right-click on the drive name of the USB stick in the Explorer window. From the menu list that appears, choose *Remove Safely* to guarantee that no data is damaged before the stick is pulled out. Once the computer has verified that all operations have safely concluded, a message will inform you that the drive may be safely removed.

Backing Up to a Hard Drive

While copying files to a USB stick or other external media is one method of backing up your information, another is to set up your computer's automatic backup. This isn't always available but, where it is, it can be a very useful way of keeping your data safe.

The popularity of external hard drives, typically connected to your main computer using USB, FireWire, or eSata cables, has risen dramatically in recent years. That's because they can store many more gigabytes of information than a USB drive and at a much lower price-per-gigabyte. And given the size of many photo and video files today, they're almost essential.

Both Apple and Microsoft have also introduced utilities to duplicate files on your computers hard disc onto an external hard drive automatically. Microsoft calls its utility Windows 7 Backup and Restore, and it is included in all versions of Windows 7. Apple calls the feature Time Machine, and it is an integral part of Mac OS X 10.5 (Leopard) and later versions.

In both cases the principle is the same; the computer will automatically back up the contents of its internal hard drive—or just the files and folders you specify—to the external drive. All you need to do is make sure that the feature is enabled and that it includes your database.

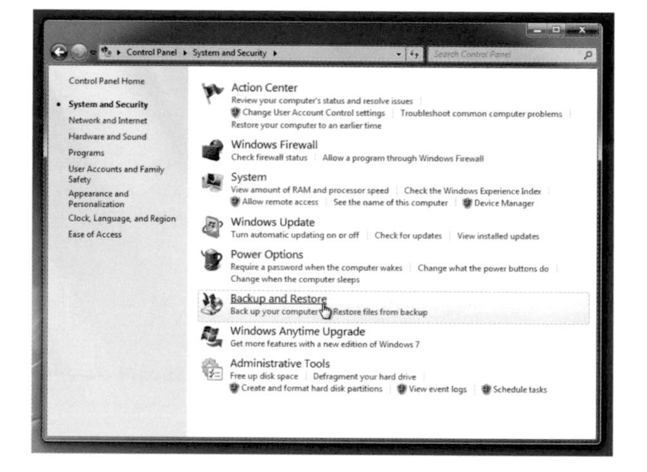

1 Be sure that your hard drive is attached to the computer using an available port, and that the cable isn't pulled too tight, which risks breaking the connection during the transfer.

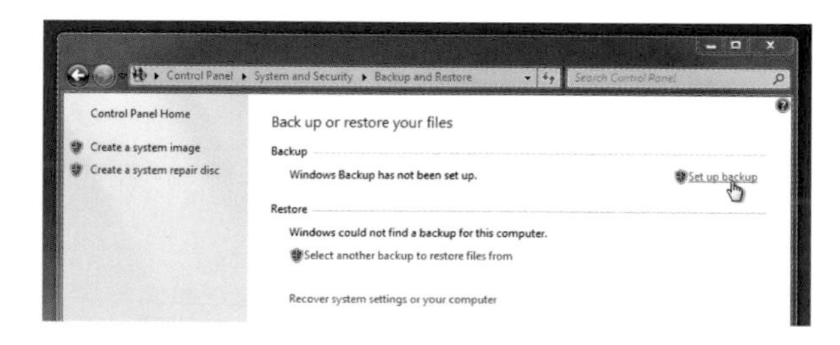

2 Locate *Backup and Restore* from the computer's *Control Panel*. This is located in the *System and Security* section. Click *Backup and Restore* to adjust your backup settings.

3 Click on the *Set Up Backup* button to be taken to a wizard (a sequence of options with on-screen explanations), which will guide you through the process of setting up automated backups. Choose your external hard drive from the list offered.

4 If you're using an external hard drive, you can back up all your data, which guarantees that your database will be included. Do this by checking the *Local Disk (:C)* option, which by default is unchecked.

5 When you've finished answering the questions, Windows will show you a summary screen. Choose the *Save Settings and Run Backup* option and, as long as you leave your additional drive attached, your computer—including *Organize Your Life*—will be backed up each week.

Time Machine for Mac

Apple's Time Machine utility is a particularly efficient automated backup feature, which backs up and stores your files hourly throughout the current day. In addition, daily backups are kept for the current month, and monthly archives are created for as many years as you have available storage capacity. When you run out of space on the backup drive, the oldest backups will be removed to make space for new ones.

1 Plug in an external hard drive, and then open the *System Preferences* panel (accessed by clicking on the *Apple* icon). Choose *Time Machine*.

2 To set up a new backup drive, click the *Select Disk* button. Your computer will automatically identify the drive you've connected and allow you to choose it from a list.

3 Next select *Options* and check that *Organize Your Life* is not on the list of excluded files.

4 Close both the *Options* and *Time Machine* windows. Backups will now begin automatically.

Online Backup

Today it is possible for you to store your computer files online, eliminating the need for any discs, USB sticks, or hard drives. Online services such as www.ibackup.com harness the speed of the Internet and use extremely fast broadband connections to backup your files to a remote computer.

An increasing number of websites now offer online storage, and many of them will provide large amounts of digital space for a fairly low fee. To back up online you will need to set up an account with a service provider and then download and install its software. Once registered, you can log in whenever you choose and back up as many files (or as few) as you wish.

The software these services use will vary between companies, but the basic steps will be the same: You need to specify which files you want to back up, and when you want them

Online data back up allows you to copy some, or all, of the files and folders on your computer to the host service's remote servers. In the event that your computer crashes, you can retrieve and restore the data. However, be careful when it comes to uploading sensitive information. Unless you are completely certain that the service is secure, it is safer not to upload your bank details or other financial details.

to be backed up. In some cases this might happen automatically, so on a daily basis your computer will contact the online service and back up your requested files, for example.

Once your data has been backed up, you can log in to your account and download any damaged or missing files if you experience a problem with your computer that results in losing some, or all, of your data. The software may even restore them to their original destination—as if they had never been missing.

However, while this is an attractive idea for nonsensitive information, it is *not* recommended as a viable option for the records you are storing in your database. Although all these online data-storage companies claim their sites are secure—and most are—do you want to trust them with information that is critically confidential, such as your finances?

Remember, computer hackers can access a lot of websites, so unless you are certain that the service you are using is fully secure, it is better to keep your personal records backed up on a CD, USB stick, or external hard drive that you can be more certain is accessible to no one other than yourself. If you already subscribe to an online back-up service, remember to make sure that your personal records are not automatically backed up or uploaded there. If you are in any doubt about how to do this, check with your service provider.

Printing

After you have entered your records, you may want to print some of them out on your home or office printer. The contact details for utility companies, for example, is the type of information that you might want to keep handy.

At the same time, some extremely sensitive data, such as your bank details and security numbers, are better off not printed. If you decide you do want to print this information out, only do so if you are certain you can keep your copies in a place that is safe from people who might use them illegally.

As a reminder, when you try and print any pages from the Safe Place section of the program, you will be asked to confirm that you want to print out these potentially sensitive records. This gives you an additional opportunity to cancel the printing process if you have pressed the *Print* button by accident.

1 Assuming you are ready to print the page you are viewing on-screen, the printing process is straightforward. On every page of the program, whether you are viewing a full record or in the list view, you will find a *Print* button at the bottom right corner of the screen.

2 When you click the *Print* button, *Organize Your Life* will open your print dialog box. The default settings for the printer have been set so that each record page will be oriented correctly (to print the pages in landscape format as they appear on your computer monitor).

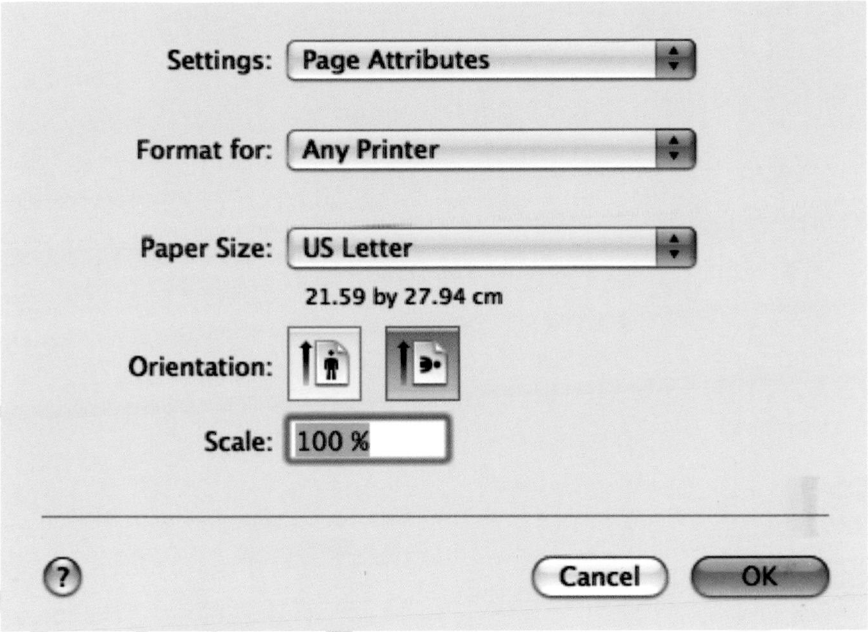

Settings: Page Attributes
Format for: Any Printer
Paper Size: US Letter
21.59 by 27.94 cm
Orientation:
Scale: 100 %
Cancel OK

Paper Size: US Letter
27.94 cm
✓ US Letter
US Legal
A4
A5
ROC 16K
JB5
B5
#10 Envelope
DL Envelope
Choukei 3 Envelope
Tabloid
A3
Tabloid Extra
Super B/A3
Manage Custom Sizes...

3 The default paper size is set to US Letter. If you will be printing on a different size paper, use the drop-down *Paper Size* option to change it. Click *OK* to print out the page you are viewing.

Saving ink

Although the records in *Organize Your Life* are in color on your computer screen, the pages you print will be made in black and white to conserve the ink in your printer cartridge. Because the records are primarily text only, you don't want your ink-jet cartridges (or toner) running out just because you are printing out color backgrounds unnecessarily.

MEDICAL
3 LEGAL
Personal
onal Data [2]
Passport number
e of issue/expiry
lace of issue
8 FINANCIAL
9 SAFE
Health Insurance Policies
Go

THE DATABASE

This chapter brings us to the heart of our subject: the database. Next you will go screen by screen through all nine categories of potential data entry, with tips on inputting your information in the appropriate fields.

Many of the fields are self-explanatory, but special features or navigational options will be pointed out as they come up in each record. Keep in mind that when you are using the program on your own, it is not necessary to progress in the linear order presented here, and you certainly don't have to fill in all the fields in every record. If certain categories are more applicable to you than others, just skip ahead—or return later—to the records that best fit your needs.

Regional Variations

As you saw on pages 30–33 (Installing the program), there are three regional versions of the database on the disc—one each for the United States, Canada, and the United Kingdom. This is because each country has different ways of dealing with certain topics covered by the program. Be sure to pick the database for your country. This book covers the specifics for the American and Canadian databases.

While all the sections of the database apply equally to the United States and Canada, the actual information you enter can differ. Taxation, for example, is mostly the concern of a federal organization in the United States as well as state agencies, but in Canada the situation varies depending on the province you live in; from federal tax only, to both federal and provincial taxes in Quebec. Similarly, health insurance can range from private medical care policies in the United States to Canada's universal health-care scheme, which is again administered on a provincial, rather than a national, level.

Each of these fundamental differences was considered when the program was developed, but for the purpose of this chapter we will be using the U.S. version of the program. Where regional changes apply, these will be highlighted, whether it is a simple change in terminology or different fields within a record. So no matter which version of the program you are using, you will know how to fill in the information that's relevant to you.

In addition, something as seemingly common as making a note of the date differs significantly: If you are in the United States, you would expect to use the format MM/DD/YYYY (month/day/year). However, in Canada you would use DD/MM/YYYY (day/month/year). While the pages that follow take their lead from the U.S. program, each version of the database has been tailored so the information you enter will be presented in the way that is most appropriate to you depending on the country you reside in.

Taxpayer ID number
IRS reference number

Taxpayer ID number
Tax Dept. reference number

The differences between the regional versions of the program range from the terminology commonly used in each country to more profound differences, such as the way taxes are implemented, and therefore, the way they are recorded in the database.

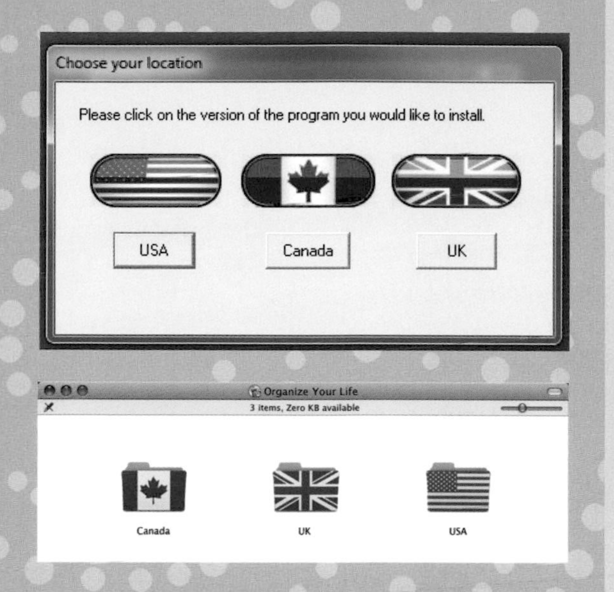

There are three regional versions of the *Organize Your Life* program on the disc—one each for the United States, Canada, and the UK. Be sure to install the correct one so that the information on the database is relevant to your country.

Common regional differences

In addition to fundamental differences in the way that the regions represented in this book deal with complex issues, such as tax or medical insurance, they also use different words or methods to describe the same thing. These have been applied to each version of the database, but to help you, the most common differences that you are likely to encounter appear below:

Date format: MM/DD/YYYY (month, day, year)	**Date format:** DD/MM/YYYY (day, month, year)
State Zip code	**Province** Postal code

1 FAMILY

Personal Data [1]

The first subject category provided in the Family section of the database is Personal Data [1]; a record for recording who you are, where you live, and other business details. This is a single record, so everything you need to add is on a single page. Most of the information listed here will be used when you want to automatically fill in future pages using the *Autofill* button. So the information may seem obvious, but entering it at the outset will save you time later.

Date of birth Enter your birth date using the format MM/DD/YYYY (two digits for the month and day, followed by four digits for the year) if you are using the U.S. program and DD/MM/YYYY for the Canadian version. For example, January 10, 1965, would be entered as 01/10/1965 in the U.S. and 10/1/1965 in Canada.

1 FAMILY 2 MEDICAL 3 LEGAL 4 EMPLOYMENT 5

Personal Data 1 | Personal Data 2

My Personal Data [1]

Name (first/middle initial/last)
Maiden/other name(s)
Date of birth
Address line 1
Address line 2
City/State
Zip/Country
Home phone (1/2)
Cell phone (1/2)
Internet phone ID (VOIP)
Personal e-mail 1
Personal e-mail 2
Facebook profile page http://www.facebook.com
Social Security number

Address The six fields you enter for your address can be automatically copied onto other screens in the database that call for this information, so you will only need to fill this in once.

Home and cell phone The home and cell phone fields allow you to enter two numbers. If you travel regularly, it can be useful to add your country codes before your personal numbers.

Internet phone ID If you have an Internet phone, such as Skype, enter the phone ID here.

Personal e-mail Once you've filled in your personal e-mail addresses, clicking on the *E-mail* icon to the right of these fields will send an e-mail to the address selected.

Facebook If you use Facebook, the social-networking site, enter the web address of your profile page here. Clicking the *Web* icon to the right of this field will open your Internet browser and take you directly to the Facebook home page. You can then log in to your Profile page.

Regional Variations

Social Security number

Social Insurance Number

6 REAL ESTATE 7 VALUABLES 8 FINANCIAL 9 SAFE PLACE

Family Members | Personal Documents

Go

My picture

Marriage status

Spouse (first/last)

Marriage date

Emergency contacts

Primary contact

Primary contact phone (1/2)

Secondary contact

Secondary contact phone (1/2)

Record created 09/12/2009; Modified 09/12/2009

PRINT QUIT

My picture You can enter a photograph of yourself by clicking on the green + icon to the right of the picture box. Only one photo can be displayed at a time, but you can change the picture whenever you want: See pages 44–45 for full instructions on how to add, remove, and view your pictures.

Marriage status When you click on this field, a downward-arrow will appear, denoting that this is a drop-down menu. Click the arrow to view the options and select your current marriage status.

Emergency contacts Here you can enter the names and phone numbers of two people who can be contacted in case of an emergency.

Print Click here to print the entire record. See page 60 for details on printing.

Personal Data [2]

The second Family screen—Personal Data [2]—provides additional categories for you to enter personal information, ranging from educational to political. Just like the previous screen, this is a single record, so there is no opportunity for adding extra pages.

Passport information You will find all the information you need to enter in this section in your passport, but it's useful to have it in the database, too. When you want to book tickets for a flight, for example, it will be easier to open the database than locate your passport.

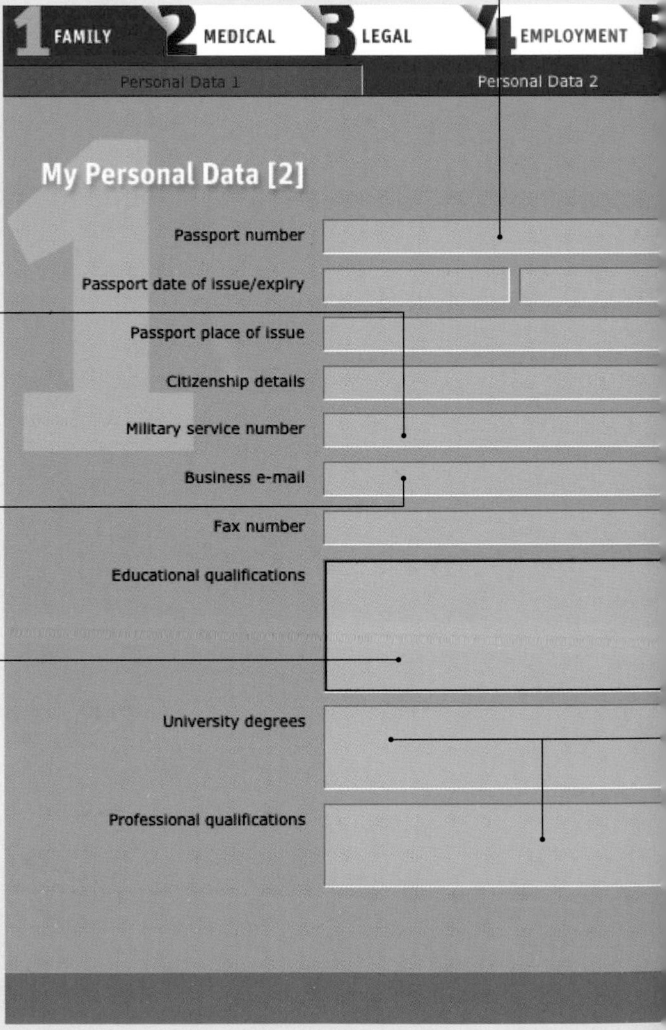

Military service number If you have served in the military, enter your service number here.

Business e-mail The field for your business e-mail includes the *E-mail* icon, which allows you to send e-mails to this address with a simple click.

Educational qualifications If you have completed any specialized courses or vocational programs to train for your field, include them here. This is the first example of a scrolling field, designated by the bar and arrows that appear at the right side of the field when you click on it. This type of field provides more space to fill with text than is visibly shown. When your text has reached the bottom of the field, continue writing until your entry is complete. To scroll through your finished text, click on the up or down arrows with your mouse or use the arrow keys on your keyboard to move the cursor up and down.

1 FAMILY 2 MEDICAL 3 LEGAL 4 EMPLOYMENT

Personal Data 1 Personal Data 2

My Personal Data [2]

Passport number

Passport date of issue/expiry

Passport place of issue

Citizenship details

Military service number

Business e-mail

Fax number

Educational qualifications

University degrees

Professional qualifications

Regional Variations

College degrees

University/ College degrees

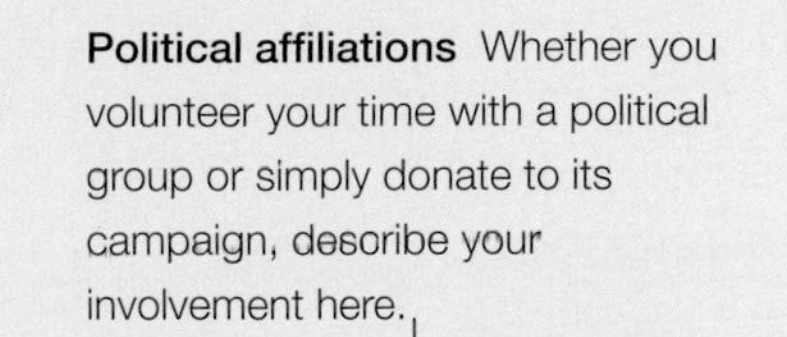

Political affiliations Whether you volunteer your time with a political group or simply donate to its campaign, describe your involvement here.

6 PROPERTY 7 VALUABLES 8 FINANCIAL 9 SAFE PLACE

Family Members | Personal Documents

Go

Professional memberships

Political affiliations

Other memberships

Personal website http://www.

Blog http://www.

Notes

Record created 09/12/2009; Modified 08/02/2010

PRINT QUIT

Personal website and Blog If you have a personal website (rather than one for your business, which will be covered later) and/or a blog, you can enter their web addresses here. Both of these fields include the *Web* icon, which you can click on to immediately open the web page in your Internet browser.

College degrees and Professional qualifications If you have received a bachelor's degree or have completed degrees at the graduate level, such as a masters', doctorate, or medical degree, enter those here. Similarly, if you have received certification to practice your field—such as passing the bar exam to be a lawyer or the Series 7 to be a stockbroker—this is the place to record it.

1 FAMILY

Family Members

The Family Members screen is where you input all your relatives' key details, from birthdays and anniversaries to contact information and photos. Where the previous two screens allowed you to create a single record only, Family Members allows you to create multiple records, so you can create a unique record for as many family members as you choose.

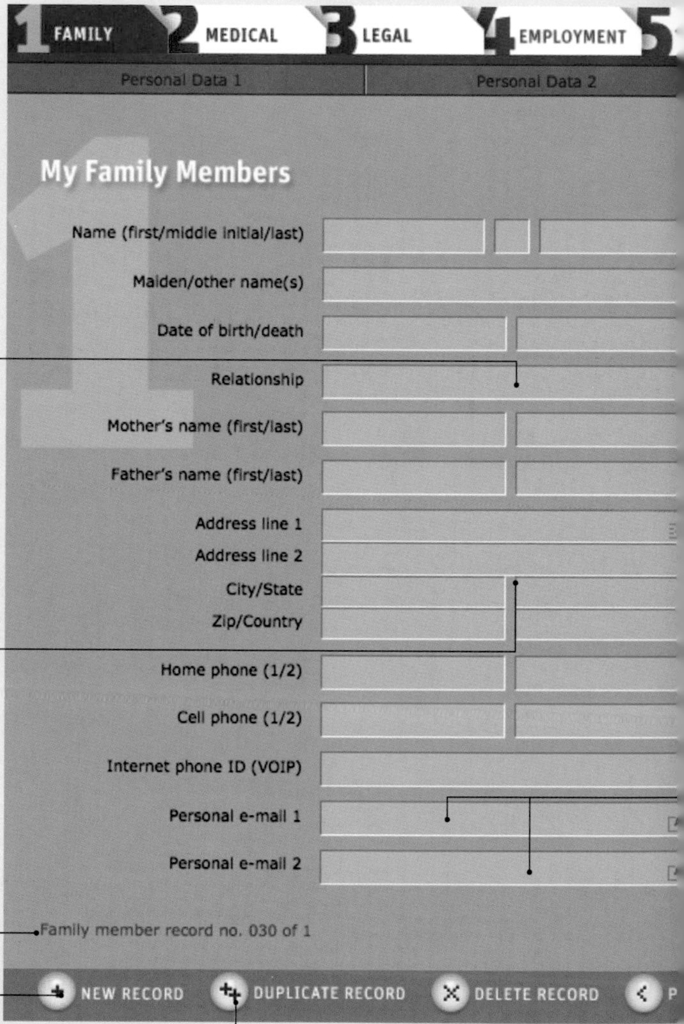

1 FAMILY 2 MEDICAL 3 LEGAL 4 EMPLOYMENT 5

Personal Data 1 | Personal Data 2

My Family Members

Name (first/middle initial/last)

Maiden/other name(s)

Date of birth/death

Relationship

Mother's name (first/last)

Father's name (first/last)

Address line 1

Address line 2

City/State

Zip/Country

Home phone (1/2)

Cell phone (1/2)

Internet phone ID (VOIP)

Personal e-mail 1

Personal e-mail 2

Family member record no. 030 of 1

NEW RECORD DUPLICATE RECORD DELETE RECORD P

Relationship This field provides a drop-down menu of relationship options, so click on it to view the selection: husband, wife, daughter, and so on. If the relationship you need isn't listed, click *Edit* at the bottom of the list. This will open a dialog box that allows you to change one or more of the default choices. Now when you click on the arrow in the Relationship field, the options will include your new entry.

Address If you live at the same address as the family member you are adding to the database, click on the *Autofill* icon. This will automatically enter the address from the Personal Data [1] record.

Family record number When creating multiple records, each one will be identified by a number. You can see the number of your current record at the bottom left.

New record Once you've completed the available fields of your first family member's record, click here to generate a new screen for another.

Duplicate record This button creates an exact copy of an existing record, which is useful if you want to create a new record that shares some information with a preexisting one. Once you create a duplicate simply edit the fields in the new record that are different than the first

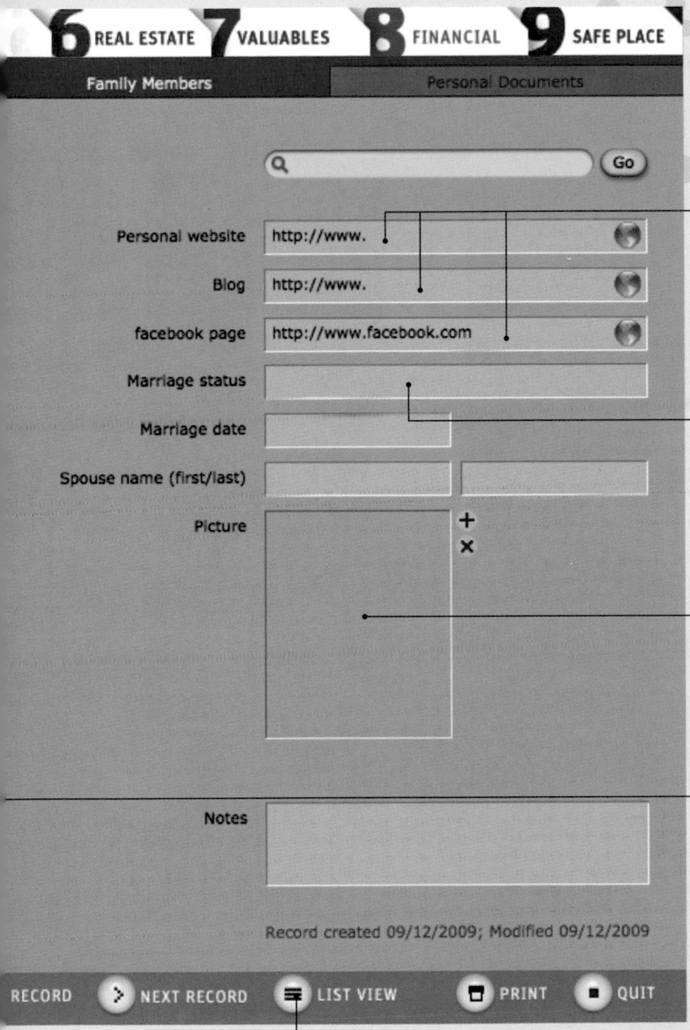

Personal website, Blog, and Facebook page All three of these web address fields include the *Web* icon to open up the specified web pages with a single click.

Marriage status This field offers the same drop-down menu of options from the first screen. From this list, select your current marriage status

Picture Add a photo of family members here. Remember that you may only include one photo for each record entered. (See pages 44–45.)

Personal e-mail Both fields for your family members' e-mail addresses include the *E-mail* icon. If you wish to send them a message, click here to open your e-mail program with a preaddressed new e-mail.

List view To view all your Family Member records at a glance, click *List View*. When shown in *List View,* records offer abbreviated information only, listing relationship, birthday, phone numbers, and e-mail.

Personal Documents

The final screen in the Family section of the database is Personal Documents. This is another multiple records screen that allows you to upload as many documents as you like. There are no rules as to what documents you can add: You might include personal documents, such as a birth certificate or marriage license, or you can add other people's documents, such as family members' passport details.

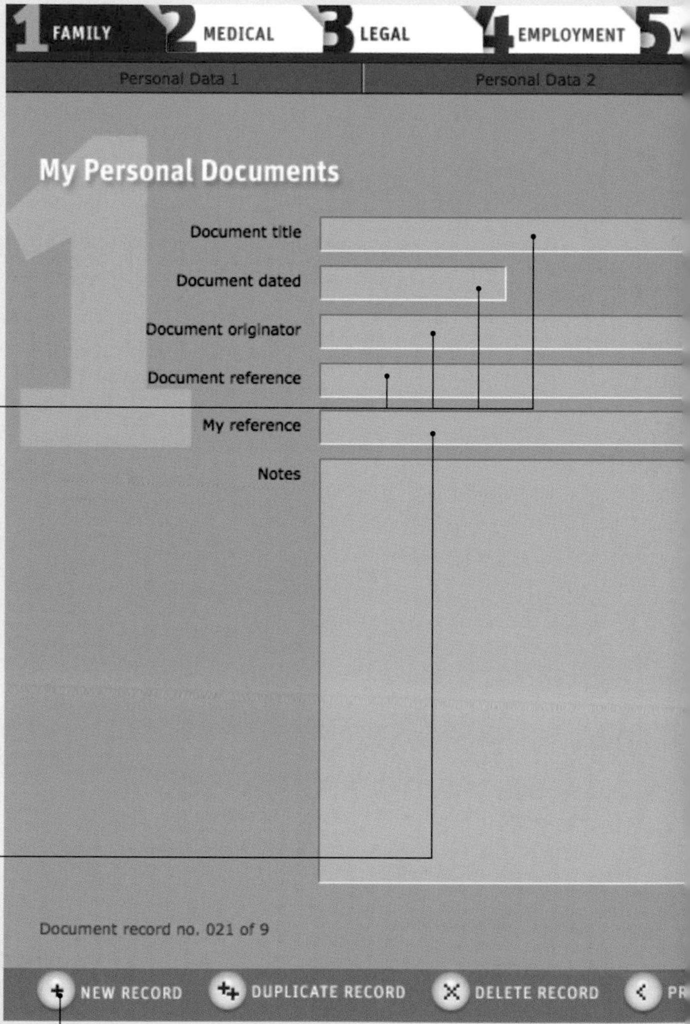

Document title, date, originator, and reference Use these fields to identify your document, when it was originated, and who created it. You can also include a document reference, such as the number or code relating to that particular document—the passport number on a family member's passport, for example.

My reference In this field you can enter a memorable reference for your document. If you were entering another family member's passport details, for example, you could use this field to make a note of whose passport it is.

FAMILY MEDICAL LEGAL EMPLOYMENT
Personal Data 1 Personal Data 2
My Personal Documents
Document title
Document dated
Document originator
Document reference
My reference
Notes
Document record no. 021 of 9
NEW RECORD DUPLICATE RECORD DELETE RECORD

New record Each record contains a single document only, so you will need to create a new record for each additional document you wish to add. After you have completed the record for your first document, click here to open a new screen for your next one.

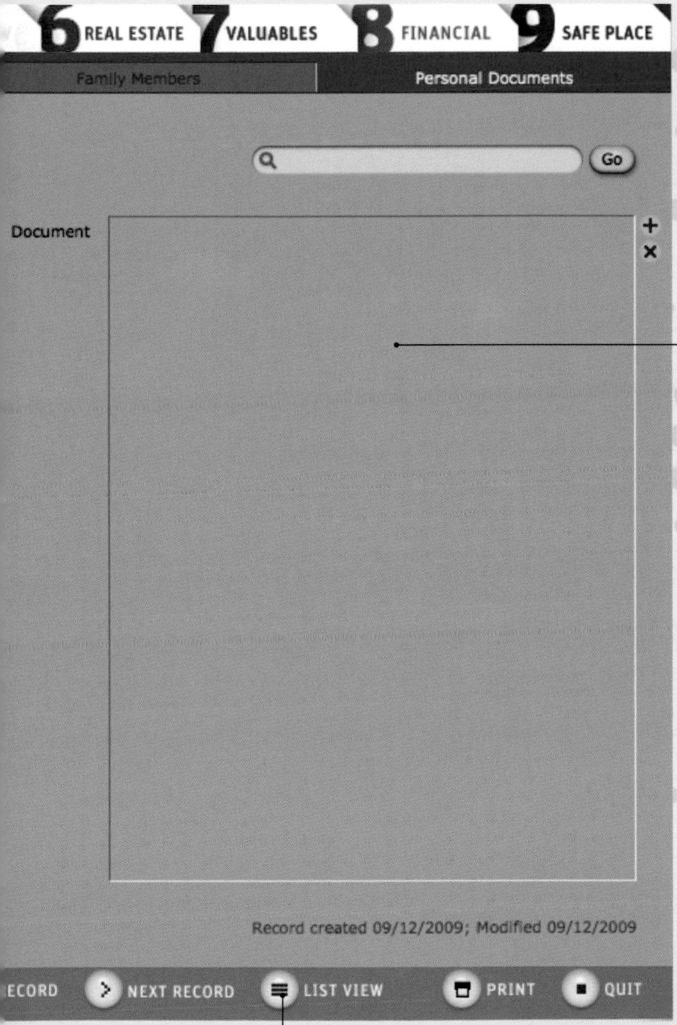

6 REAL ESTATE 7 VALUABLES 8 FINANCIAL 9 SAFE PLACE

Family Members | Personal Documents

Go

Document

Record created 09/12/2009; Modified 09/12/2009

ECORD NEXT RECORD LIST VIEW PRINT QUIT

Document In addition to describing the document at the left of the record, you can also import a copy of the actual document for easy reference. For more information on scanning and saving documents, see pages 18–25.

List view Once you've finished adding as many, or as few, documents as you choose, you can see them at a glance by clicking the *List View* button.

2 MEDICAL

Medical Contacts

In the second category, Medical, the first screen is Medical Contacts, in which you can enter physicians' main details. This is a multiple records screen, so you may include as many medical contacts as you choose. For a quick look at all your physicians with their specialties and phone numbers, click *List View*.

Physician direct line and cell phone Space is provided for two direct phone lines, as well as two cell phone numbers.

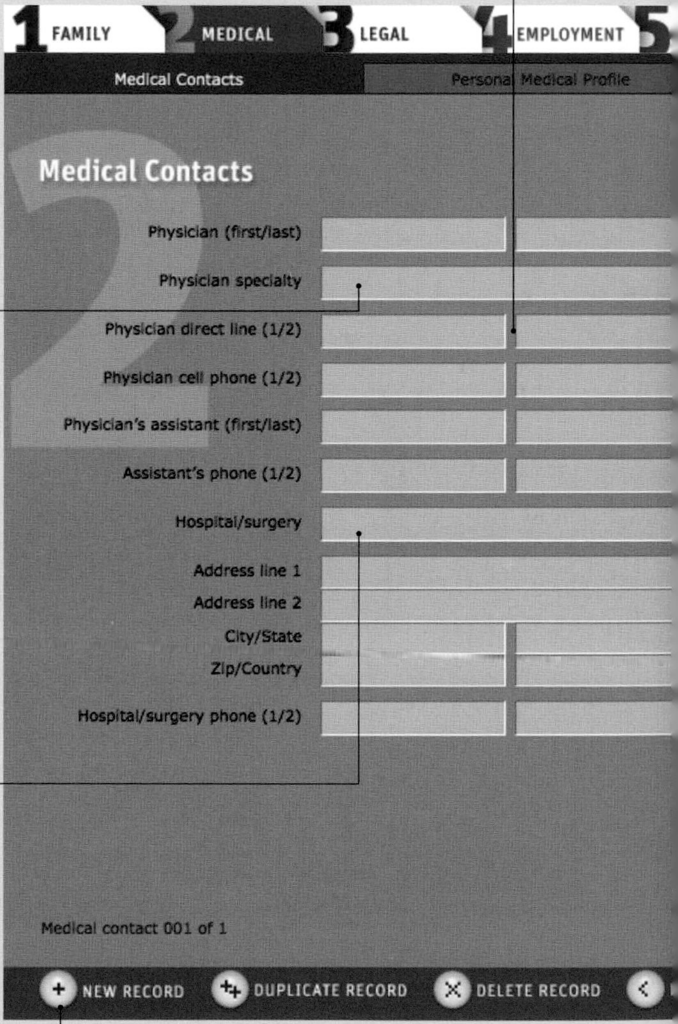

Physician specialty This field contains a drop-down menu of various medical specialties, such as chiropractor and optometrist. If you wish to add a specialty that is not shown, choose *Edit* from the drop-down list. You may add as many others as needed and can also delete any items on the list. When you are satisfied with your changes, click *OK*. Now when you call up the drop-down menu, your additional option(s) will appear on the list.

Hospital/surgery If your physician is affiliated with a certain hospital or surgery, enter the details here, including the name of the hospital/surgery, the address, and the phone number. Again there are two fields for the phone number, so you can include a main and alternate phone line.

New record To create new records for additional physicians, click here. If they are affiliated with the same hospital or surgery, you may want to choose *Duplicate Record* instead, so you don't have to retype the address.

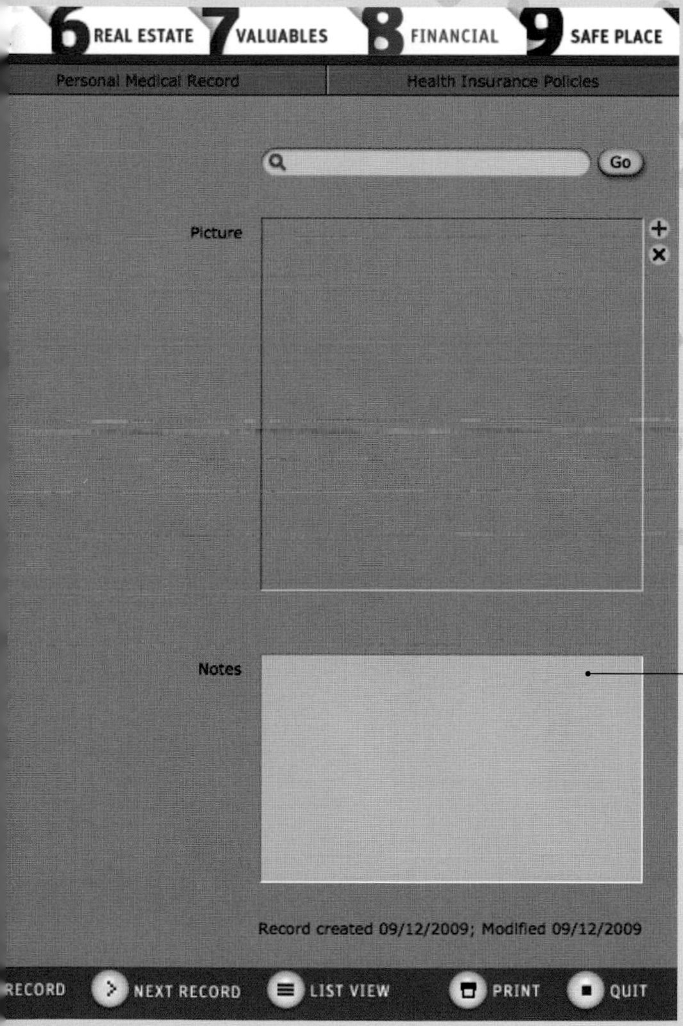

6 REAL ESTATE 7 VALUABLES 8 FINANCIAL 9 SAFE PLACE

Personal Medical Record | Health Insurance Policies

Go

Picture

Notes

Record created 09/12/2009; Modified 09/12/2009

RECORD · NEXT RECORD · LIST VIEW · PRINT · QUIT

Notes You can use this scrolling field to record any other information about your physician or your surgery.

2 MEDICAL

Personal Medical Profile

The second screen in the Medical records section is Personal Medical Profile. This is the place for the details of your personal health, such as medical conditions, allergies, and medications. Note that this is a single record screen, so you will need to enter all your pertinent information in the given fields, rather than creating separate records for specific items.

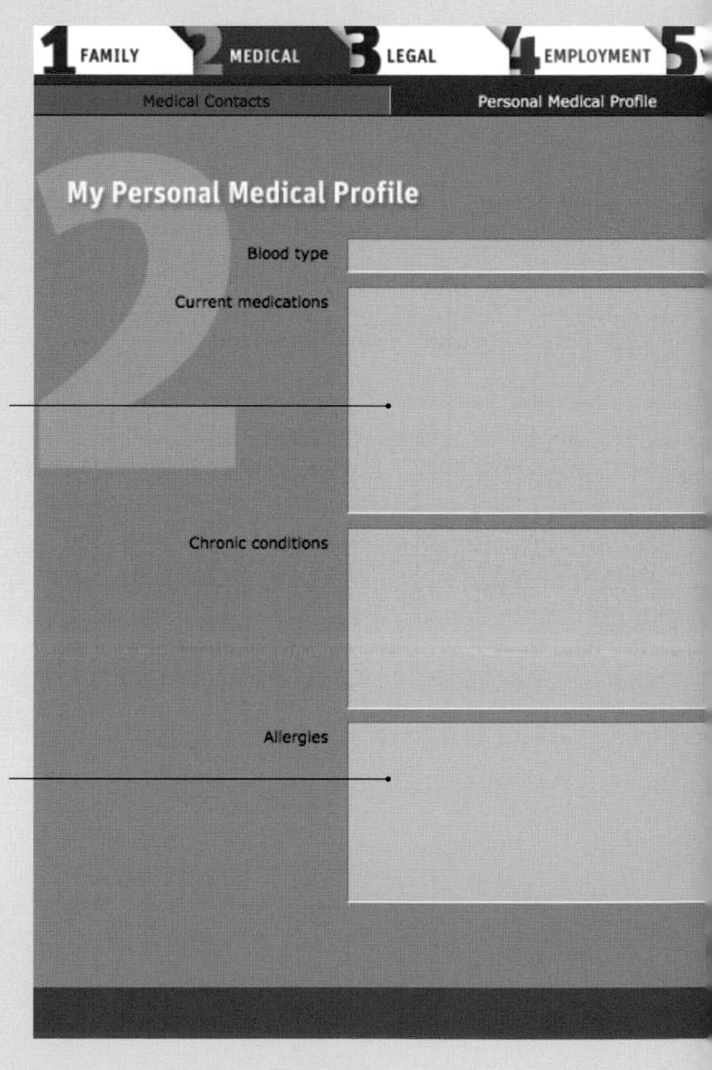

Current medications Enter any medications you take regularly. Some useful details you may want to include are the brand and generic name, dosage, dates for refills, and expiration dates.

Allergies People with allergies can potentially have a long list of triggers, including foods, plants, and different types of animal hair. If this applies to you, entering them here is an efficient way to keep track of what to avoid in your daily life. You might also describe what type of allergic reactions you have and how they should be treated.

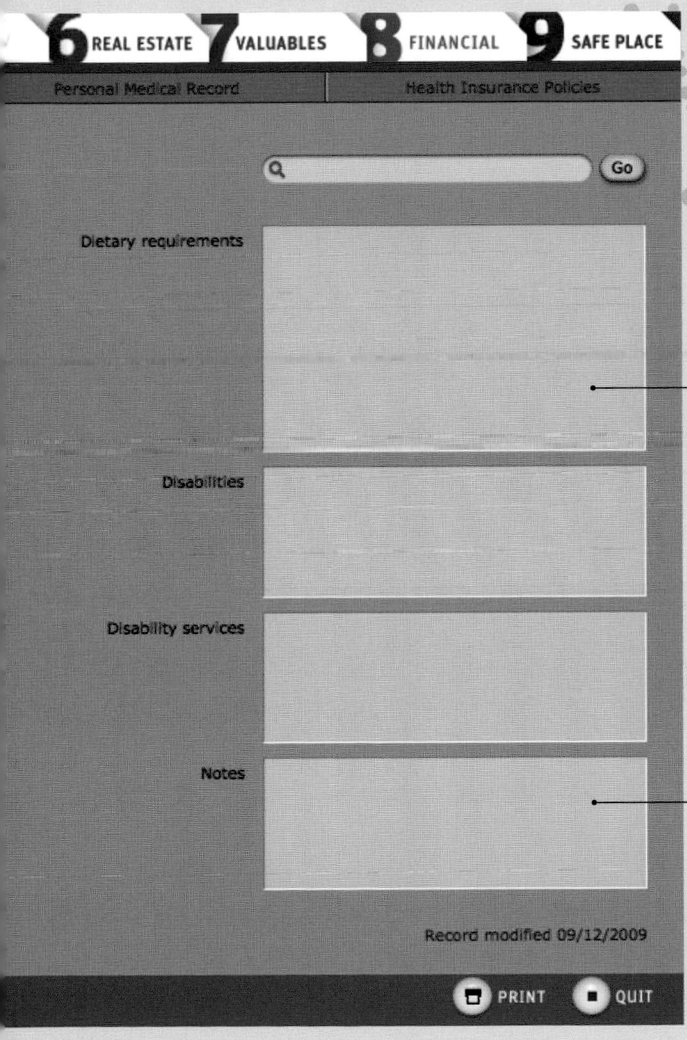

6 REAL ESTATE 7 VALUABLES 8 FINANCIAL 9 SAFE PLACE

Personal Medical Record | Health Insurance Policies

Go

Dietary requirements

Disabilities

Disability services

Notes

Record modified 09/12/2009

PRINT QUIT

Dietary requirements If you have any specific dietary restrictions, you can enter that here.

Notes If you would like to include any additional information or comments beyond those covered here, such as the addresses of useful websites on different medical conditions, allergies, or disabilities, you may add them here. You could also enter useful contact details, such as the phone number of your local pharmacy.

3 LEGAL

Legal Contacts

The first screen in the Legal category is Legal Contacts. This is where you can record the details of your legal counsel, from contact information to your lawyers' responsibilities. This is a multiple records screen, so if you use more than one lawyer, you may enter a separate record for each. Click *List View* for a full list of your lawyers' firms, specialties, and phone numbers.

Attorney, Specialty, and Company Use these fields to enter the name of your attorney, their specialty area, and the name of their company.

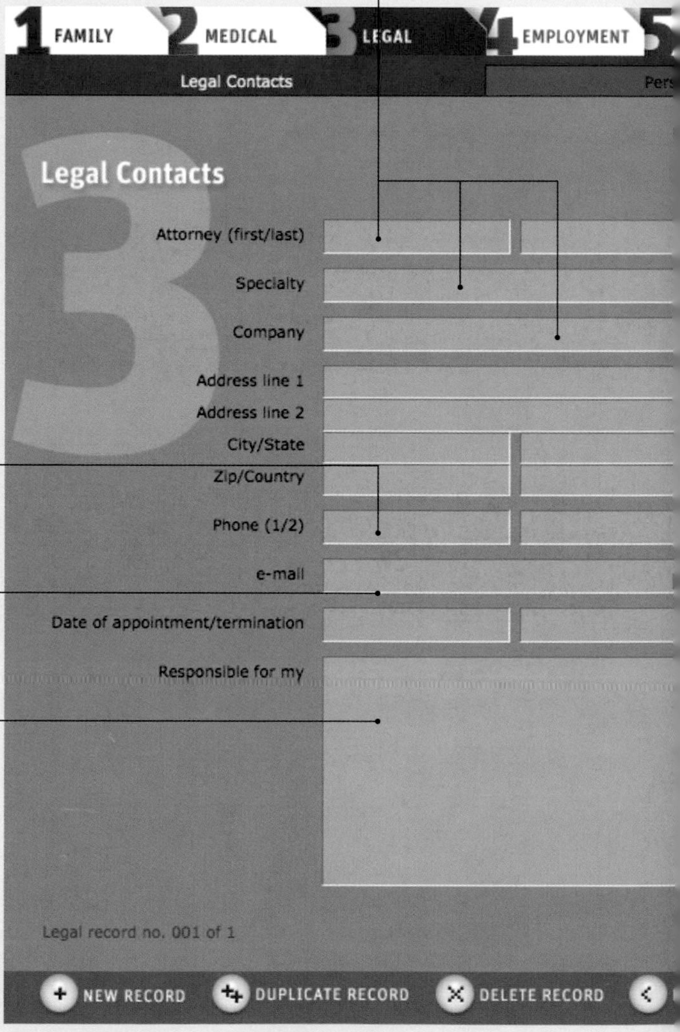

1 FAMILY 2 MEDICAL 3 LEGAL 4 EMPLOYMENT 5

Legal Contacts

Legal Contacts

Attorney (first/last)

Specialty

Company

Address line 1

Address line 2

City/State

Zip/Country

Phone (1/2)

e-mail

Date of appointment/termination

Responsible for my

Legal record no. 001 of 1

NEW RECORD DUPLICATE RECORD DELETE RECORD

Phone Two fields are provided for phone numbers, so you can enter both your lawyer's direct line and the firm's general number.

E-mail Click on the E-mail icon at the end of the field to send an e-mail directly to your lawyer.

Responsible for my Here you can describe the nature of your lawyer's work for you, such as negotiations with different parties, drawing up agreements, reviewing documents, and so on.

Regional Variations

Attorney

Lawyer

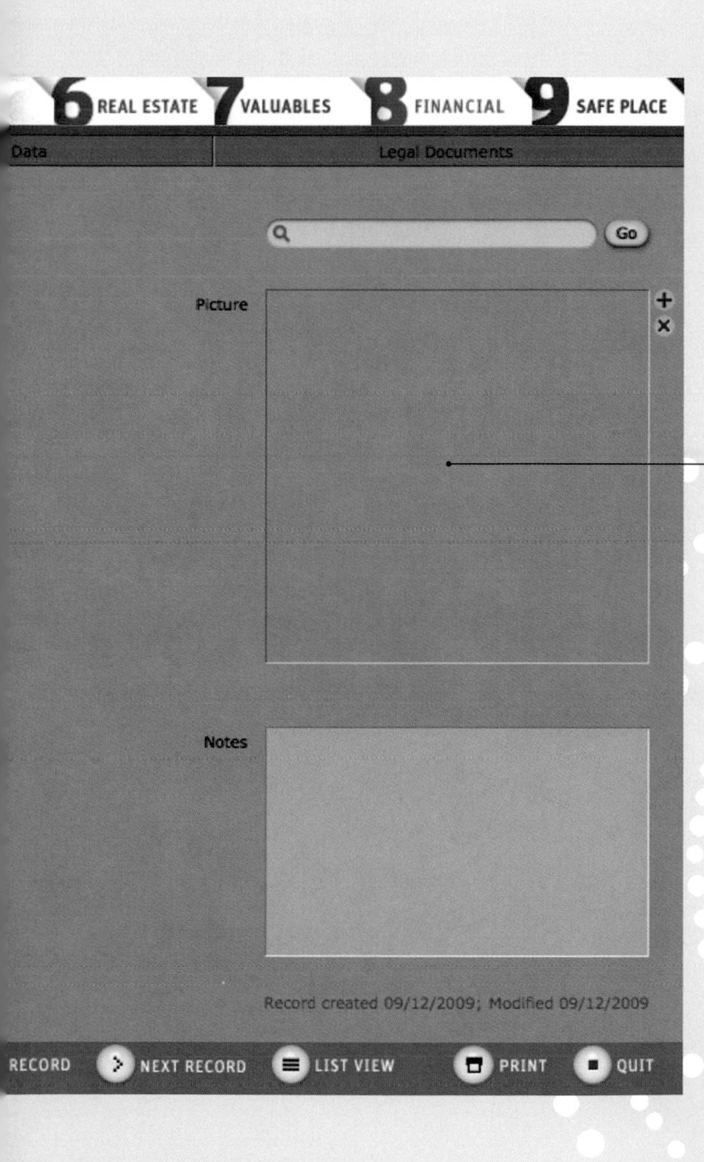

Picture If you'd like this record to include a photograph related to the legal issue—such as a person, place, object, or document—you can include it here.

3 LEGAL

Personal Legal Data

The second Legal screen is Personal Legal Data, covering the details of your legal arrangements, such as wills, trust funds, divorces, and so on. This is a single record screen, so all the pertinent information needs to be entered in the fields provided. If at any point you wish to make changes to your original data—you have decided to change beneficiaries of your estate, for example, or you are adding a new codicil to your will—simply delete the obsolete information from a field and enter the updated version in its place.

Will details Note here your main intentions for the future of your estate.

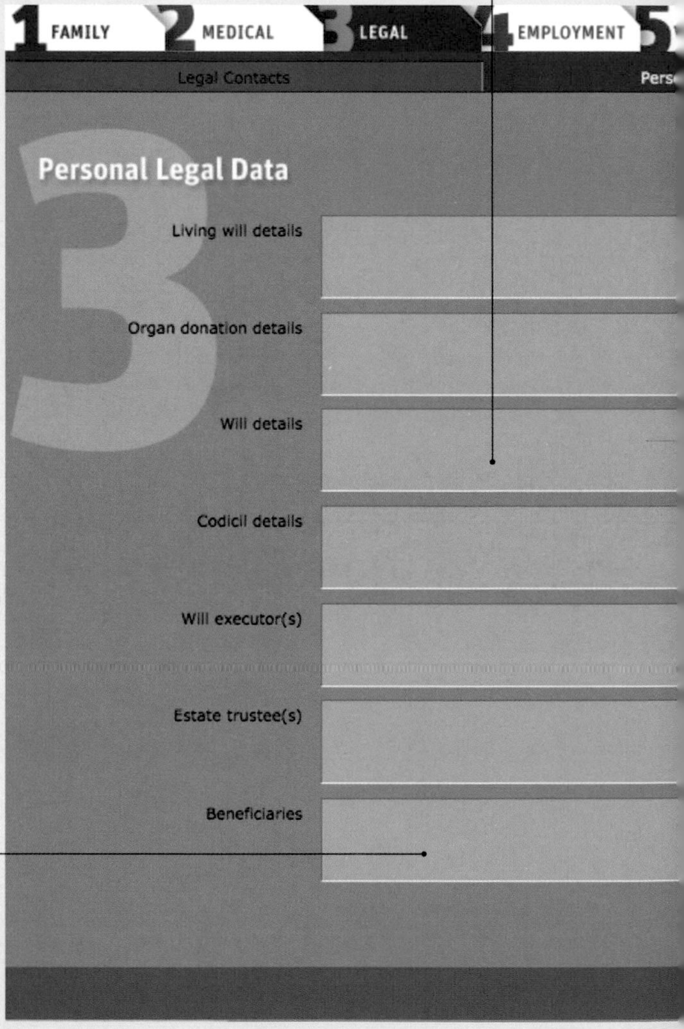

1 FAMILY 2 MEDICAL 3 LEGAL 4 EMPLOYMENT 5

Legal Contacts

Personal Legal Data

Living will details

Organ donation details

Will details

Codicil details

Will executor(s)

Estate trustee(s)

Beneficiaries

Beneficiaries If you have multiple beneficiaries, including family, friends, or colleagues, list them here along with the funds, property, and so on, that you intend to bequeath to them.

6 REAL ESTATE 7 VALUABLES 8 FINANCIAL 9 SAFE PLACE

Data

Legal Documents

Go

Guardianship(s)

Trust funds

Trust fund beneficiaries

Trust fund trustee(s)

Funeral plans

Power of attorney

Divorce details

Record created 09/12/2009; Modified 09/12/2009

PRINT QUIT

Trust funds If you have set up any trust funds, list their contents and explain their purpose.

Trust fund beneficiaries List the beneficiaries of any trust funds and what they contractually receive—either at present or a future date.

Divorce details Enter significant items, such as a financial arrangement made with a former spouse and whether you are making regular payments or receiving certain sums.

tip:

All the fields on this screen are scrolling fields. So even though this is a single record screen, there is plenty of room to enter information on each topic. However, many of these subjects are potentially lengthy, so just enter the most important points as a quick reference.

Current Employment Details

The first screen in the Employment category is your Current Employment Details, where you can record the most basic data regarding your work—generally, the nature and place of your employment, along with your earnings.

1 FAMILY 2 MEDICAL 3 LEGAL 4 EMPLOYMENT 5

Current Employment Details | Current

Employment Details: Employed

Employed

Employer

Division/Branch

Job title

Job description

Start date

Employee number

Address line 1

Address line 2

City/State

Zip/Country

Main phone

Direct line

Employment type The first field is a drop-down menu, which offers a list of employment types: employed, self-employed, limited liability company owner, and incorporated business owner. Choose the one that applies to you to bring up a record screen that is appropriate to that employment type. Here we will look at the Employed page—the other types are covered on the following pages.

Employment details The left side of the Employed page is fairly self-explanatory; you can enter straightforward facts, such as the name and address of your employer, your position at the company, your start date, and employee number.

tip:

If your employment situation fits more than one of the options available in the Employment type drop-down menu, you can fill out more than one employment record.

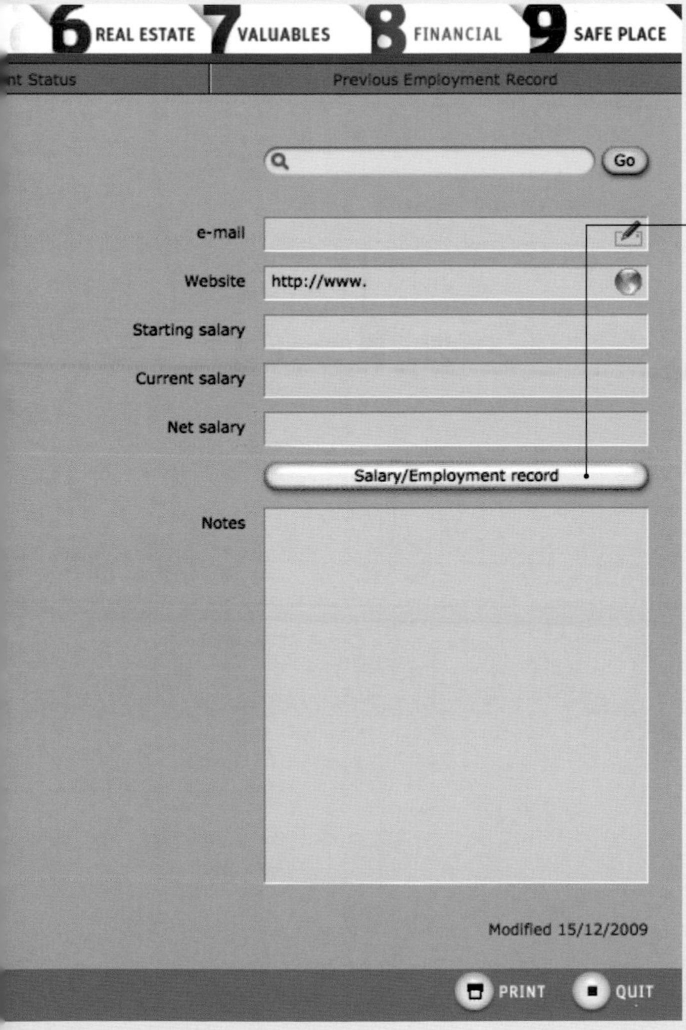

Salary/Employment record This button opens up a separate screen that lists your employment history and salaries at different employers.

This screen resembles the *List View* format, but while a *List View* displays only a portion of the information previously entered on a full record page, you can enter the text directly into this space. This should be treated as a separate record from the Current Employment Details screen, because some of the information you'll add is shown here only. For example, if you have switched job roles or locations with your employer, which has affected your salary, you might enter these details. Clicking the *Back to Record* button at the top right of the screen will return you to the Current Employment Details record.

→

4

EMPLOYMENT

Current Employment Status

This page allows you to list the types of benefits you may receive through your current employment, from health and unemployment to retirement and union benefits. This is a single record screen, but most of the fields are scrolling fields, permitting you to enter more text than the visible capacity.

1 FAMILY 2 MEDICAL 3 LEGAL 4 EMPLOYMENT 5

Current Employment Details | Current

Employment Status

Retirement benefits

Health benefits

Family/medical leave benefits

Federal contract benefits

Other benefits

Compensation programs

Unemployment insurance

Vacation time

Maternity/paternity leave

Retirement benefits If your position provides a pension after a certain number of years of service, enter that information here. Be sure not to confuse this with your 401k, which will be covered on the Pension screen of the Financial section.

Health benefits If your employer provides you with health benefits, input the name and plan of the insurance company. If you have not already done so, create a full record for this insurance on the Health Insurance Policies screen in the Medical section of the database.

Other benefits If you have additional benefits from your employer that are not covered on this screen, such as additional time off because your office closes during Christmas week, enter those benefits here.

Regional Variations

Unemployment insurance	Employment Insurance
Maternity/ paternity leave	Parental leave

6 REAL ESTATE 7 VALUABLES 8 FINANCIAL 9 SAFE PLACE

nt Status | Previous Employment Record

Go

Professional development

Union membership details

Union membership benefits

Notes

Modified 15/12/2009

PRINT QUIT

Union membership details and benefits If you belong to a union, you may be entitled to additional benefits, so be sure to enter the details of both your union membership and the benefits here.

5 VEHICLES

Driver Profile

The first screen in the Vehicles category is the Driver Profile. On this screen you can enter information on your current driving status, from details about your driver's license to any offenses you may have on your record.

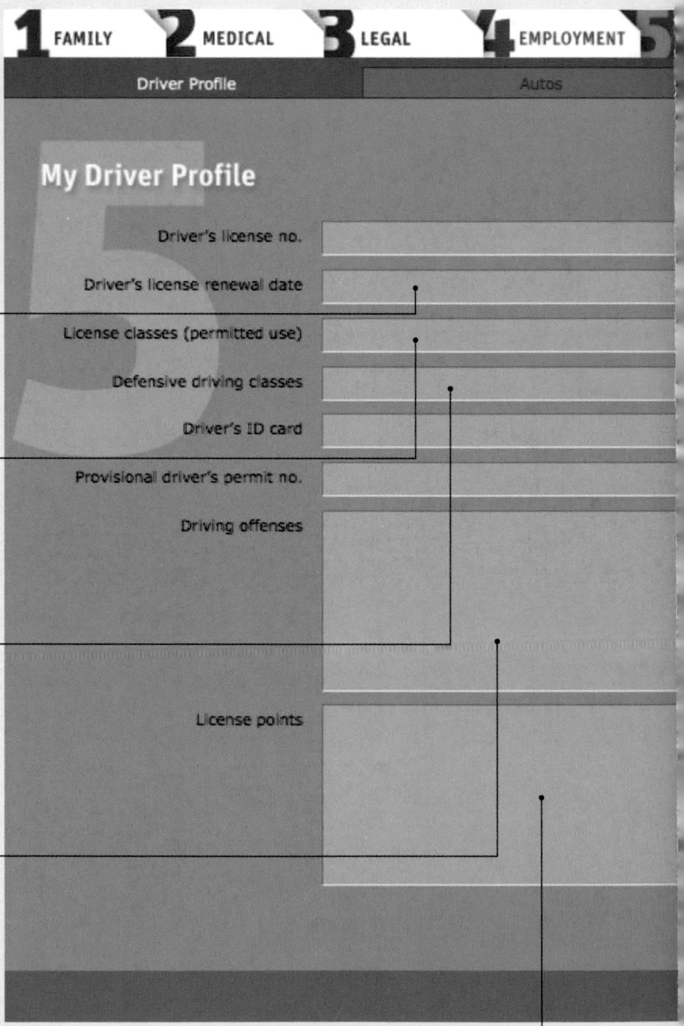

1 FAMILY 2 MEDICAL 3 LEGAL 4 EMPLOYMENT 5

Driver Profile | Autos

My Driver Profile

Driver's license no.

Driver's license renewal date

License classes (permitted use)

Defensive driving classes

Driver's ID card

Provisional driver's permit no.

Driving offenses

License points

Driver's license renewal date Don't get caught with an expired license: Enter your renewal date here as a useful reminder.

License classes Use this field to list the types of vehicle your license permits you to drive—perhaps you are entitled to ride a motorcycle, as well as a car, for example.

Defensive driving classes If you have completed a defensive driving class, or an advanced driving course, this is the field where you can enter the details.

Driving offenses If you've received speeding tickets, parking fines, or committed any other offenses, keep track of them here.

License points Keep track of any points you have received on your driving record here.

Regional Variations

License points

Demerit points

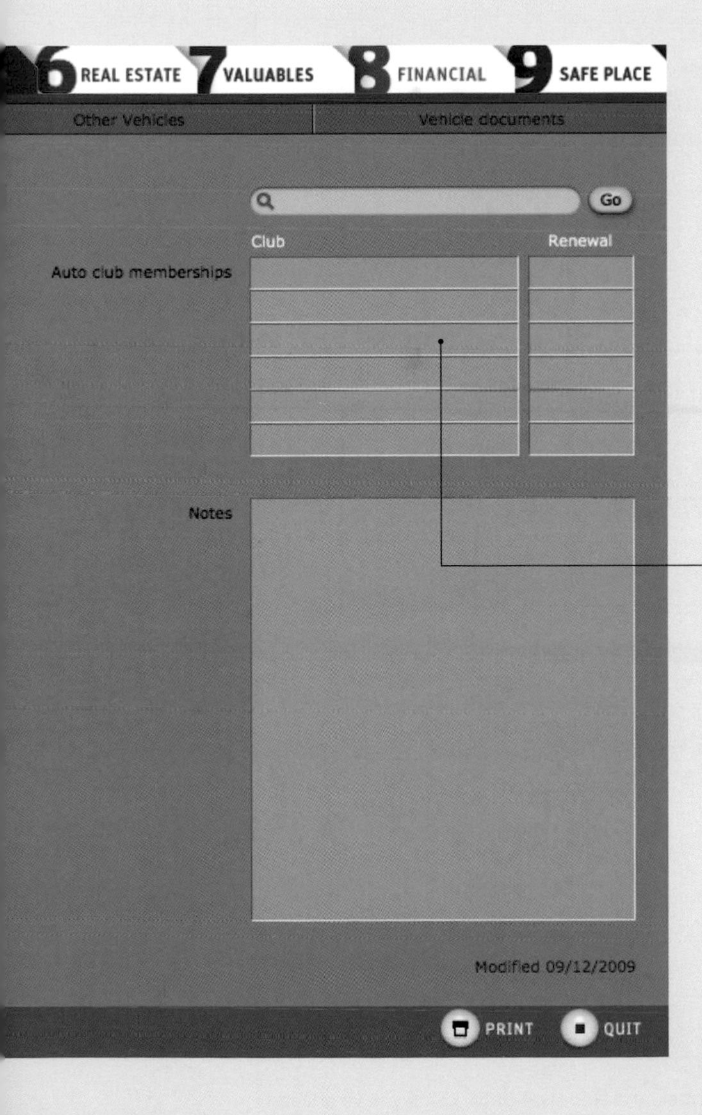

Auto club memberships Whether you aspire to purchase the newest Ferrari or collect classic cars, you may belong to associations for the automobile enthusiast.

If applicable, you could also include membership to a breakdown/recovery service, adding the recovery service's contact details in the *Notes* field below.

5

VEHICLES

Other Vehicles

If you own other vehicles beyond a car—such as a motorcycle, truck, RV, or boat—you can enter pertinent information about them on this page. This is a multiple records screen so you can create a record for each vehicle you own or have owned in the past. Not surprisingly, the fields on this screen are very similar to those on the Autos screen.

Alternative vehicle This is a drop-down menu providing a range of vehicles you might own, from a bicycle to an RV. To add additional vehicles not shown, choose the Edit option to add a new vehicle type to the list.

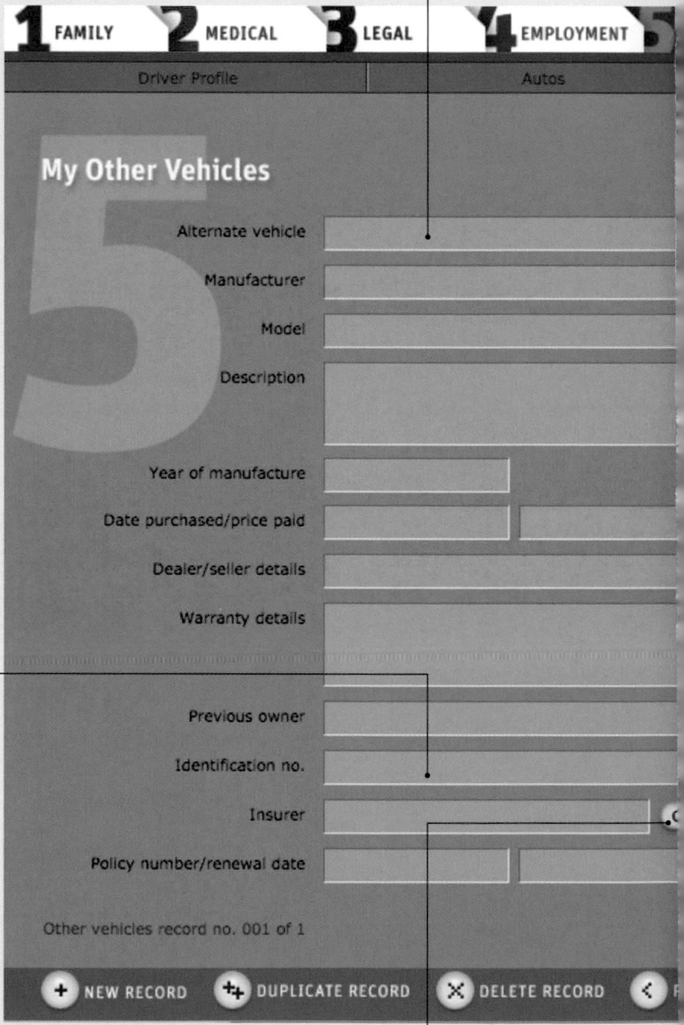

Identification number Depending on the vehicle you have, the identification number will differ. It could be the license number on a motorcycle, for example, or the frame number on a bicycle.

Go The *Go* button takes you to the Vehicle Insurance screen where you can add additional insurance details. That screen also lists insurance for cars as well as any other type of vehicles you may own.

6 REAL ESTATE 7 VALUABLES 8 FINANCIAL 9 SAFE PLACE

Other Vehicles
Vehicle documents

Go

Modifications

Service schedule

Security details

Date sold/sale price

Purchaser

Notes

Images

Record created 09/12/2009; Modified 09/12/2009

RECORD NEXT RECORD LIST VIEW PRINT QUIT

Security details If your vehicle has a security device, such as an alarm or immobilizer, you can enter the make and model of the system in this field.

Date sold/sale price If you sell your vehicle, enter the date you sold it, and the price you received for it here.

Images You can add up to four photographs of your vehicle, which can be useful if you ever decide to sell it.

5 VEHICLES

Vehicle Documents

On the Vehicle Documents screen you can upload any important papers you have that are related to your car, boat, motorcycle, and so on. These might include a warranty, an instruction manual, or a bill of sale. This is a multiple records page so you may upload as many documents as necessary. However, this is not the place for your insurance documents; those need to be uploaded to the Vehicle Insurance page in the Finance section.

Document title Remember that you may only upload one document per record, but you can create multiple records. If you wish to add another document, click *New Record* on the bottom menu bar to create a blank record.

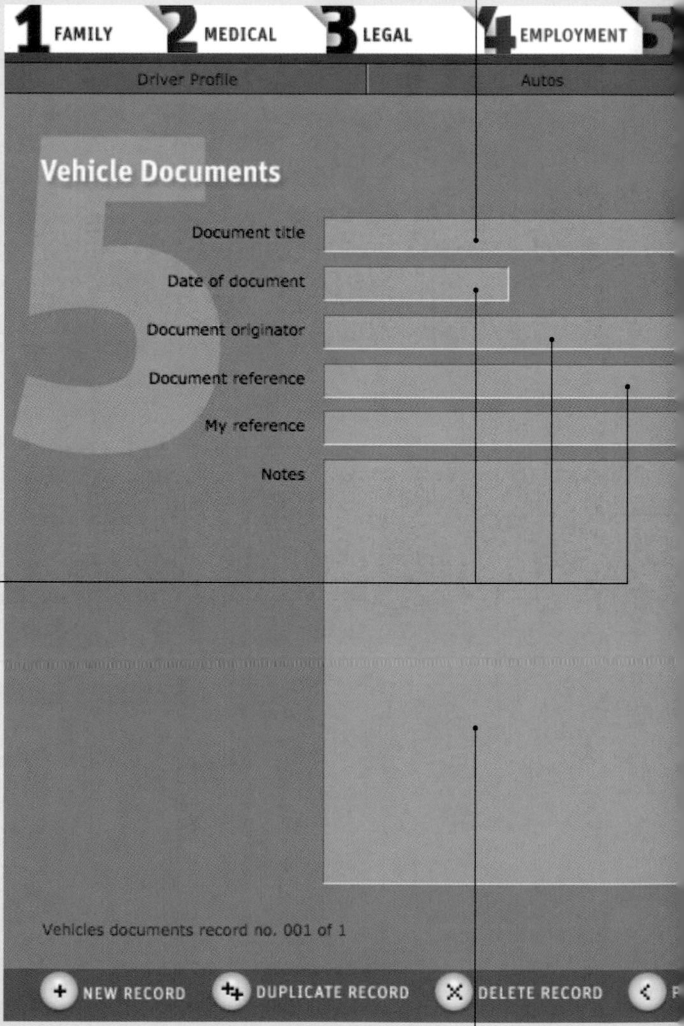

1 FAMILY 2 MEDICAL 3 LEGAL 4 EMPLOYMENT 5

Driver Profile | Autos

Vehicle Documents

Document title

Date of document

Document originator

Document reference

My reference

Notes

Vehicles documents record no. 001 of 1

NEW RECORD DUPLICATE RECORD DELETE RECORD

Date of document, Document originator, and Document reference For each document, you are provided with fields for important reference information, such as the date the document was created and who or where it originated.

Notes Use the *Notes* field to highlight any important points in your documents that you would like to see at a glance.

6 REAL ESTATE 7 VALUABLES 8 FINANCIAL 9 SAFE PLACE

Other Vehicles | Vehicle documents

Go

Document

Record created 09/12/2009; Modified 09/12/2009

RECORD NEXT RECORD LIST VIEW PRINT QUIT

Document You can import a copy of the document for easy reference. To add a document click on the green + button. If you wish to change or update the document, click on the red x to delete the current file, then click the green + to add the new one. See pages 18–25 for more information on documents and images.

Property Utility Locations

On this screen you can enter the location of the various utilities within your home, such as your water supply, gas meter, and heating and cooling controls. The left side of this single record page contains all of the common utilities—simply enter their location in the relevant field. In case of any malfunction or need for adjustment, it's important to identify where these can be found at a moment's notice.

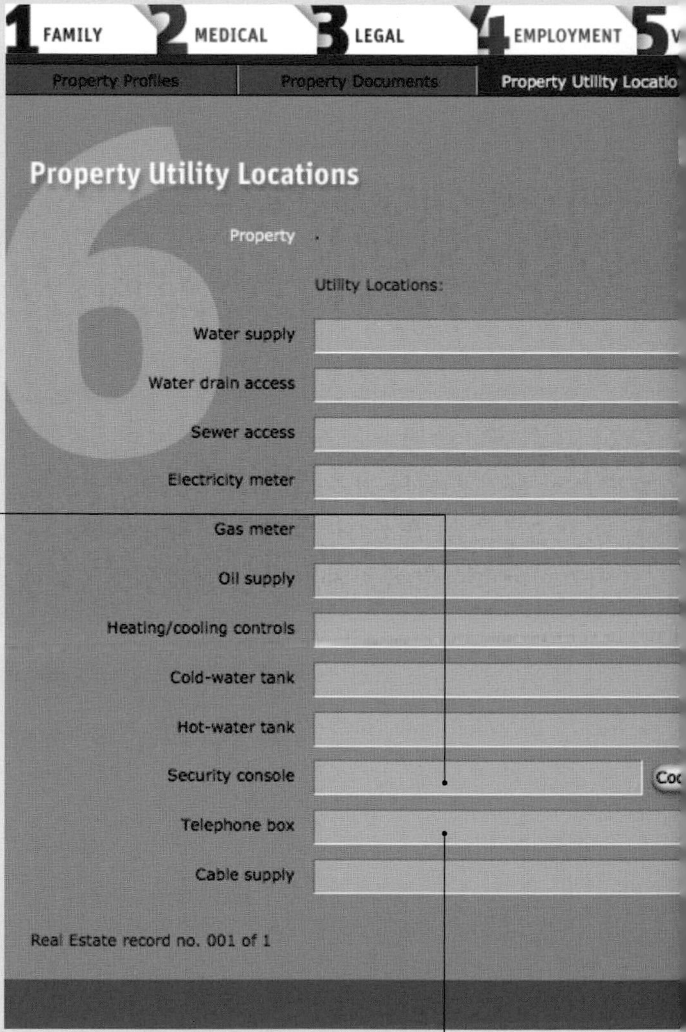

Security console If you have one, this is the control panel of your property's security system where you enter a personal code. Only enter the location of the device here—the code itself goes in Safe Place. To quickly navigate to the relevant page in the Safe Place section, click the *Code* button. To ensure the confidentiality of the data stored in Safe Place, you will be asked to enter your password before this screen appears.

Telephone box This is the location of your phone's primary distribution box, to which all phone extensions throughout your home are connected.

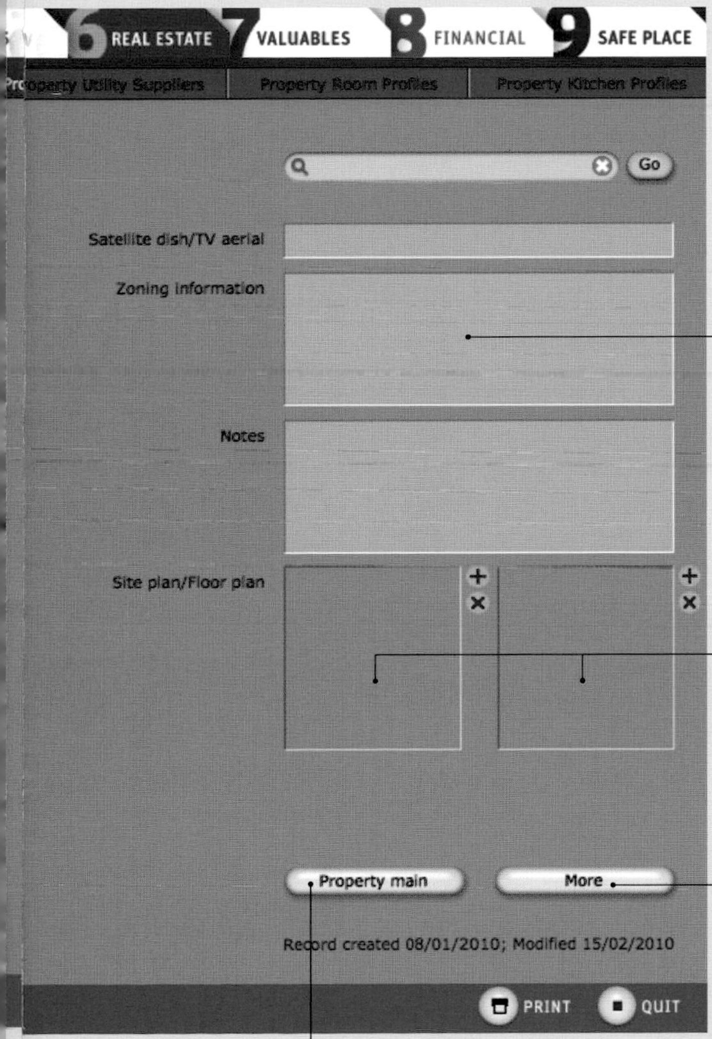

Zoning information If you plan to build additions to your property, zoning requirements and restrictions need to be carefully reviewed before beginning construction. In this field you can enter key points for your reference.

Site plan/Floor plan Whether your property consists of multiple structures or a single building or apartment, you will likely have a site or floor plan, or possibly both. You can upload these documents here so they are readily available.

More Click here to move on to the Property Utilities screen.

Property main Click here to return to the main Property Profiles screen.

8 FINANCIAL

Stocks

The financial section opens with a screen devoted to your investments in stocks. This is a multiple record screen, so you may create a separate record for each stock in your portfolio. You can click on the *List View* button to see, or print, your entire stock portfolio on a single sheet.

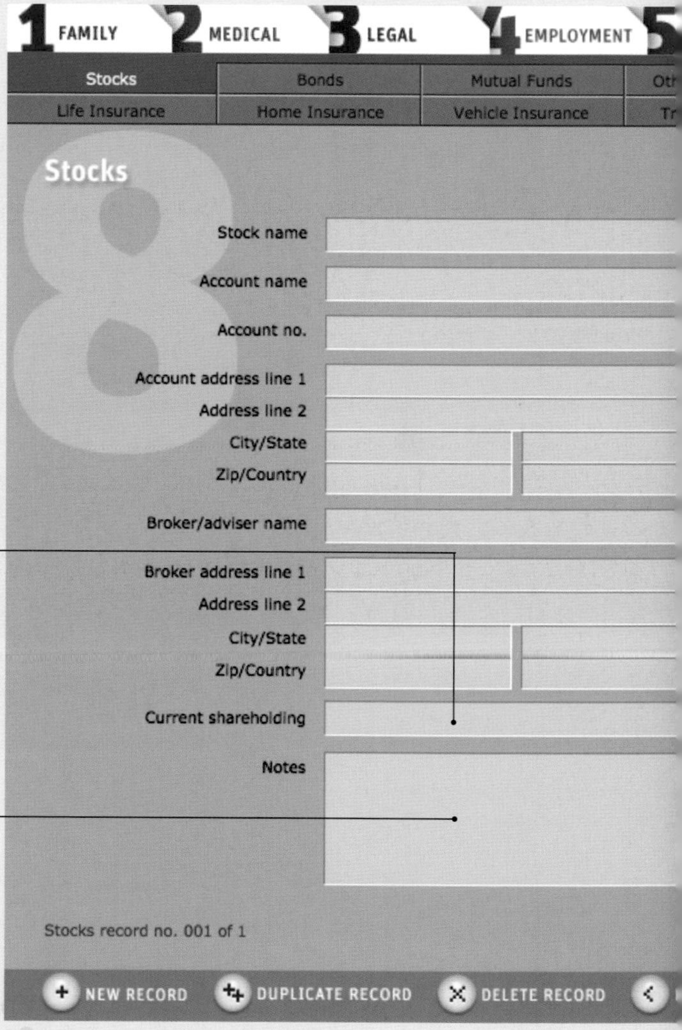

1 FAMILY 2 MEDICAL 3 LEGAL 4 EMPLOYMENT 5

Stocks | Bonds | Mutual Funds | Oth
Life Insurance | Home Insurance | Vehicle Insurance | Tr

Stocks

Stock name
Account name
Account no.
Account address line 1
Address line 2
City/State
Zip/Country
Broker/adviser name
Broker address line 1
Address line 2
City/State
Zip/Country
Current shareholding
Notes

Stocks record no. 001 of 1

NEW RECORD DUPLICATE RECORD DELETE RECORD

Current shareholding This figure will be calculated automatically from the two numbers you have entered in the right hand column for Shares purchased and Shares sold.

Notes If your stock pays a dividend, you can enter that information here.

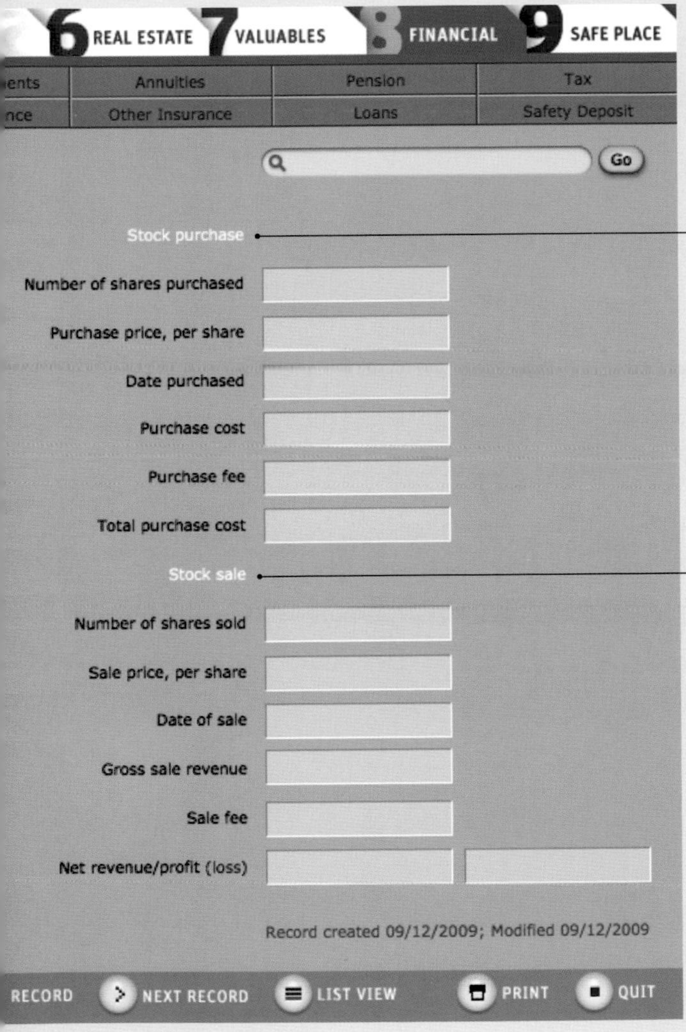

6 REAL ESTATE 7 VALUABLES 8 FINANCIAL 9 SAFE PLACE

ents | Annuities | Pension | Tax
nce | Other Insurance | Loans | Safety Deposit

Go

Stock purchase

Number of shares purchased

Purchase price, per share

Date purchased

Purchase cost

Purchase fee

Total purchase cost

Stock sale

Number of shares sold

Sale price, per share

Date of sale

Gross sale revenue

Sale fee

Net revenue/profit (loss)

Record created 09/12/2009; Modified 09/12/2009

RECORD NEXT RECORD LIST VIEW PRINT QUIT

Stock purchase Under the Stock purchase heading you can enter the number of shares you have purchased and the price per share. With this information, the program will automatically fill in the Purchase cost field. When you add the Purchase fee, the Total purchase cost field will be updated, too.

Stock sale Just like the Stock purchase section, the program will save you from making any calculations for yourself: Simply enter the number of shares sold and the sale price to determine your gross sale revenue.

Next enter a sale fee to generate your net revenue. The figure given in the left field is your total net revenue, while the right field will display your total profit—shown in black—or your loss, in parentheses in red.

8 FINANCIAL

Bonds & Mutual Funds

If your financial portfolio includes bonds or mutual funds, you may enter the pertinent details on these screens. This includes account and broker information, as well as the dates and prices of purchase and sale. Again, these are multiple records screens to allow for ownership of multiple bonds or mutual funds. The screen shown at right is the Bonds screen—the Mutual Funds page is fundamentally the same.

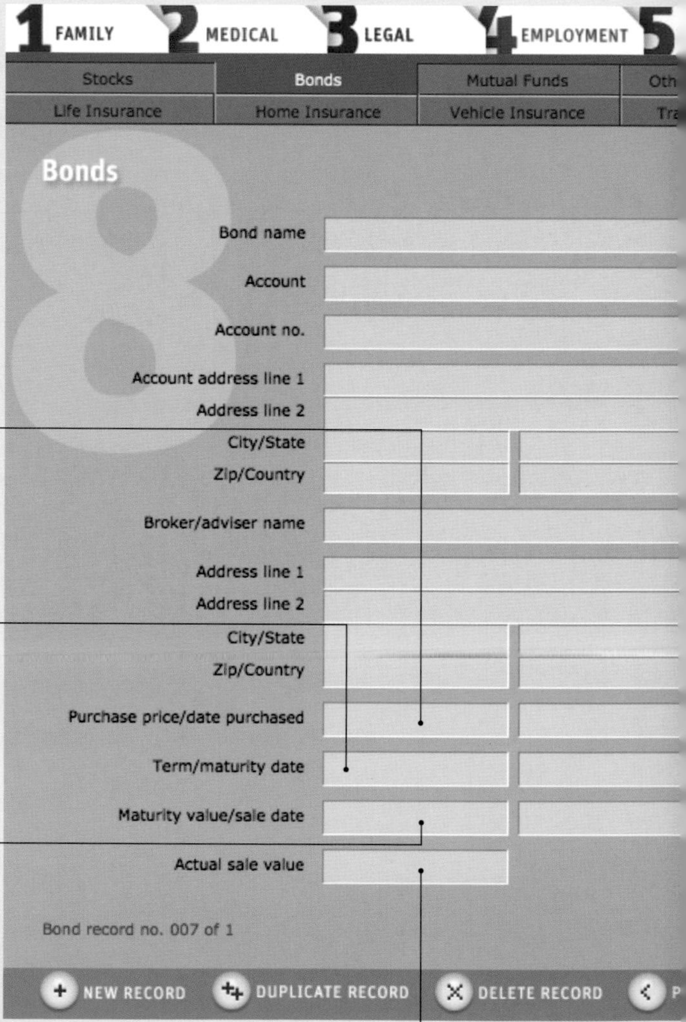

Purchase price/date purchased For your Bonds this is the price of the bond, and for Mutual Funds it is the Purchase cost: The total amount of money you have invested in a particular fund.

Term/maturity date In the left field you can enter the term of the bond or fund, or the length of time for which it is valid—5 years, 10 years, and so on. In the right field, enter the end date of the term.

Maturity value/sale date Use the left field to enter the value of your bond or fund when it matures. If you have already sold it, enter the date of your sale in the right field.

1 FAMILY 2 MEDICAL 3 LEGAL 4 EMPLOYMENT 5

Stocks | Bonds | Mutual Funds | Oth
Life Insurance | Home Insurance | Vehicle Insurance | Tra

Bonds

Bond name
Account
Account no.
Account address line 1
Address line 2
City/State
Zip/Country
Broker/adviser name
Address line 1
Address line 2
City/State
Zip/Country
Purchase price/date purchased
Term/maturity date
Maturity value/sale date
Actual sale value

Bond record no. 007 of 1

NEW RECORD DUPLICATE RECORD DELETE RECORD P

Actual sale value Enter the price at which you sold the bond or fund, for comparison against the maturity value.

Notes This field might include the rate of interest paid on your bond or the risk level and past performance of a fund.

List view You can get an at-a-glance look at all your bond or fund records by using the *List View* button. This can also be useful if you want to print a list for easy reference.

8 FINANCIAL

Other Investments

Beyond stocks, bonds, and mutual funds, your investments might take many other forms, such as stock futures and options, private equity, currencies, or commodities, such as precious metals or oil. To accommodate a range of diverse investments, this is another multiple records screen. If you are investing in property, however, the details should not be entered here, but on the Property Profiles screen in Real Estate.

Description and Details There are no fixed criteria for what is and isn't an investment—it is up to you to decide what you want to include on this page. Use the Description and Details fields to provide information about the investment.

1 FAMILY 2 MEDICAL 3 LEGAL 4 EMPLOYMENT 5

Stocks | Bonds | Mutual Funds | Oth
Life Insurance | Home Insurance | Vehicle Insurance | Tr

Other Investments

Name
Description
Details
Account name
Account no.
Account address line 1
Address line 2
City/State
Zip/Country
Broker/adviser name
Broker address line 1
Address line 2
City/State
Zip/Country

Other investments record no. 001 of 1

NEW RECORD DUPLICATE RECORD DELETE RECORD

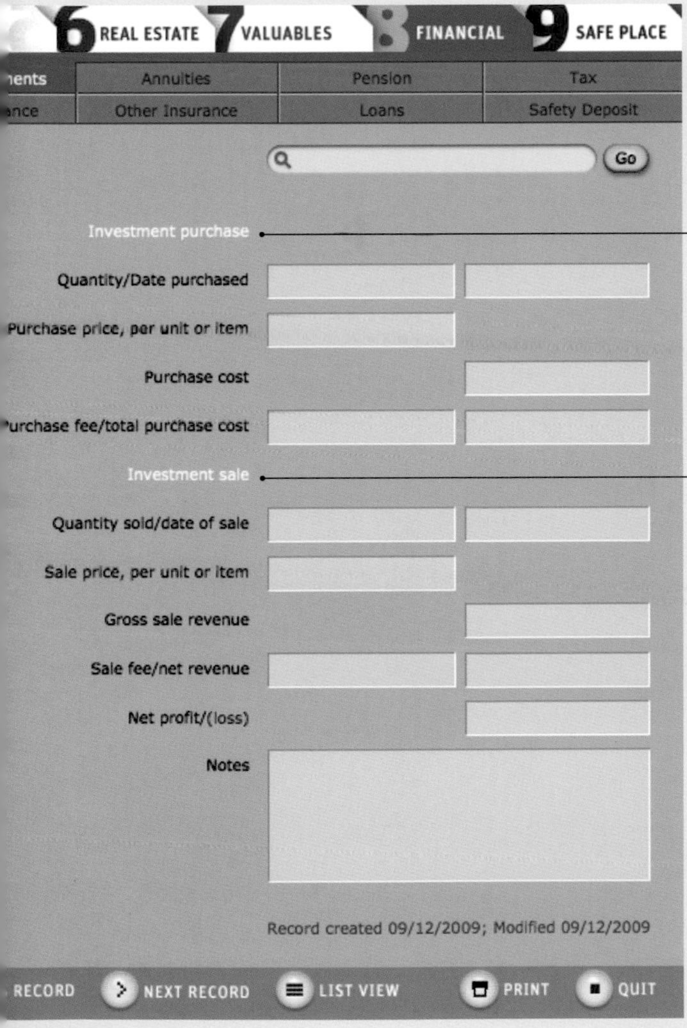

Investment purchase Start detailing your investment by entering the number of units purchased—whether that is measured in weight or volume or by individual item. Once you have entered a quantity, you can enter the price per unit or item; your purchase cost is automatically calculated. Finally, add the fee charged for the transaction to determine your total purchase cost.

Investment sale If you sell an investment, you can enter the relevant information here. Enter the quantity sold and the sale price to have the program determine automatically your gross sale revenue, and add any sale fees to calculate the net profit (or loss) in the next-to-last field.

8 FINANCIAL

Annuities

If you receive annuities of any kind, they should be documented on this screen. Your annuities might be issued by various sources ranging from an insurance company or CD (Certificate of Deposit) to a trust fund or divorce settlement. This is a multiple records screen that provides for as many annuities as you receive. To view the key information from all your records, just use the *List View* button at the bottom right of the page.

Annuity and Amount/Payment intervals Use these fields to identify which annuity the record relates to, the amount it pays, and the frequency of those payments.

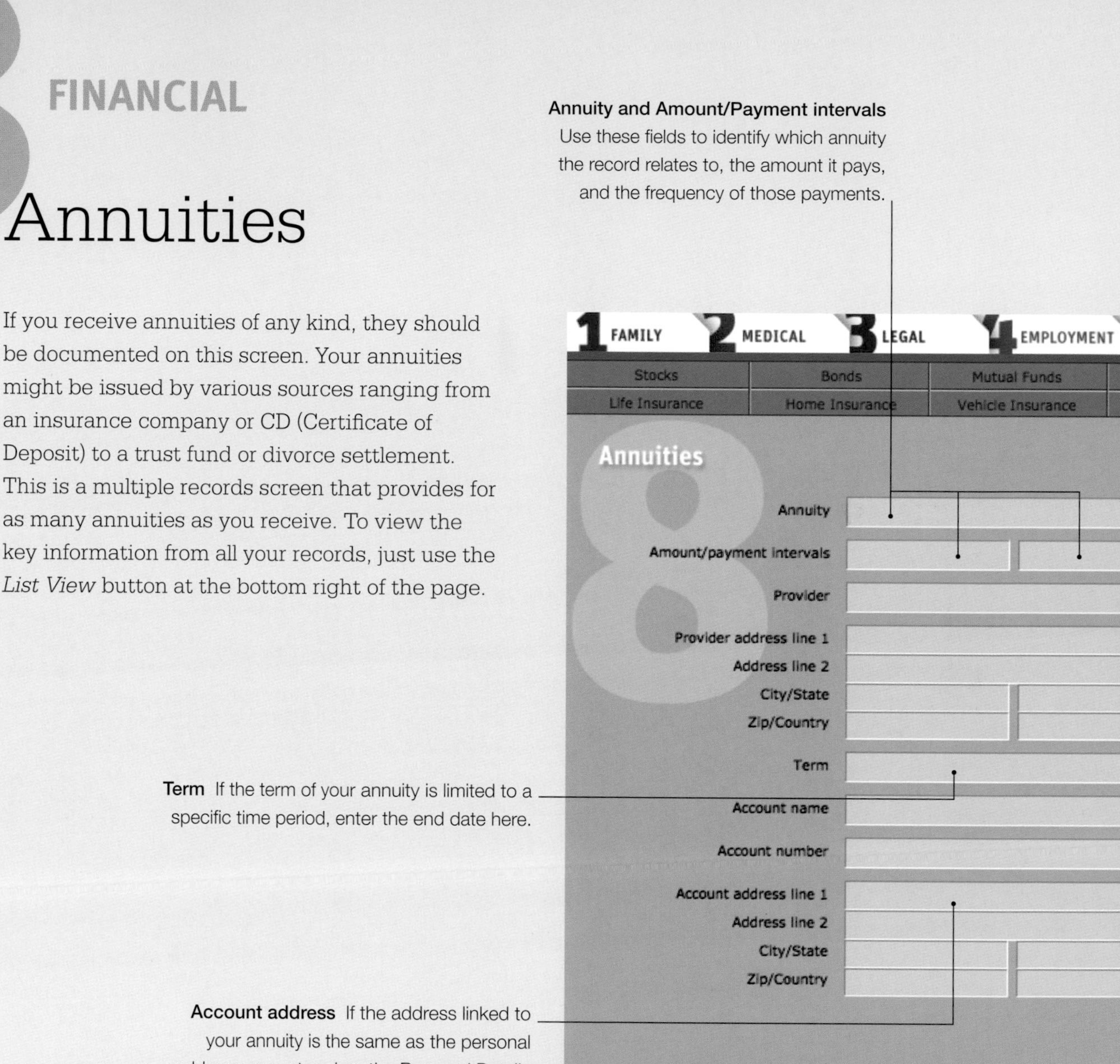

Term If the term of your annuity is limited to a specific time period, enter the end date here.

Account address If the address linked to your annuity is the same as the personal address you entered on the Personal Details page, simply click the *Autofill* icon to duplicate that information here.

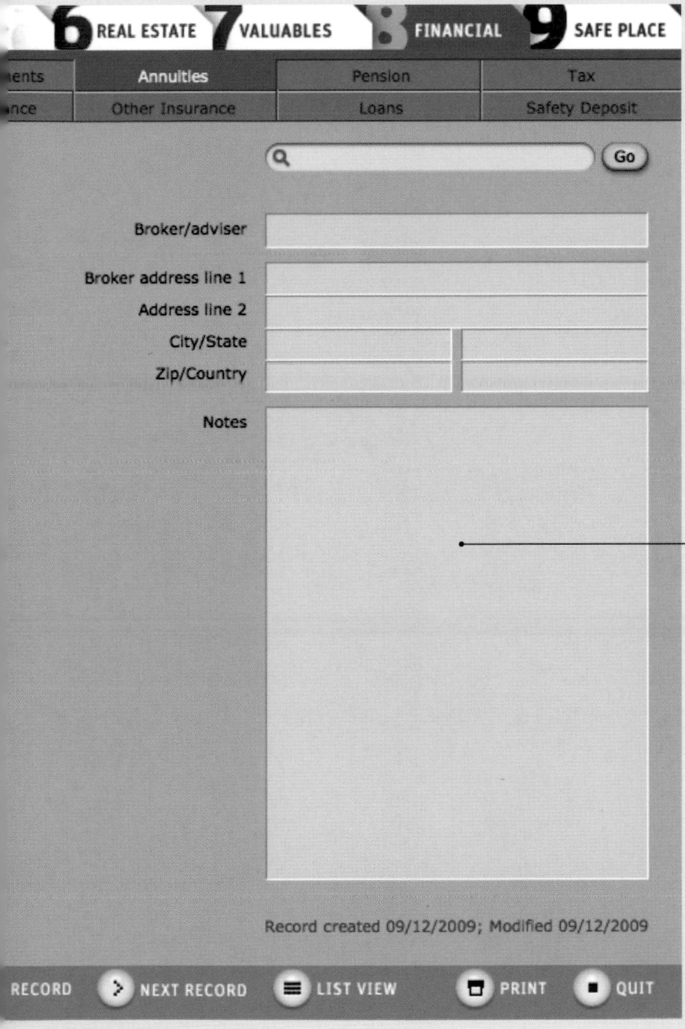

ents | Annuities | Pension | Tax
nce | Other Insurance | Loans | Safety Deposit

Broker/adviser

Broker address line 1

Address line 2

City/State

Zip/Country

Notes

Record created 09/12/2009; Modified 09/12/2009

RECORD NEXT RECORD LIST VIEW PRINT QUIT

6 REAL ESTATE 7 VALUABLES 8 FINANCIAL 9 SAFE PLACE

Notes If the terms of your annuity include any provisions or requirements, you can add a reminder here.

8 FINANCIAL

Pension

Pensions come in many forms, whether they are set up by an employer, union, government agency, or created by you independently. In any case, this screen allows you to add the important details. If you receive pensions from multiple sources, you can create a separate record for each one.

Plan type If you have been a full-time employee at a company in the United States, you probably have a 401k pension plan. Whether you are self-employed or work for someone else, you may also have set up an Individual Retirement Account (IRA). Depending on your age and number of years worked, you will be entitled to payments from Social Security, too.

1 FAMILY 2 MEDICAL 3 LEGAL 4 EMPLOYMENT 5

Stocks | Bonds | Mutual Funds | Oth
Life Insurance | Home Insurance | Vehicle Insurance | Tra

Pensions

Account name
Plan type
Term/date of maturity
Provider name
Account number
Provider address line 1
Address line 2
City/State
Zip/Country
Custodian/broker name
Custodian address line 1
Address line 2
City/State
Zip/Country

Pensions record no. 001 of 1

NEW RECORD DUPLICATE RECORD DELETE RECORD

Regional Variations

Government pension: Because everyone over the age of 65 is part of a federal public pension plan in Canada (provincial in Quebec), an additional field is provided in the Canadian version of the database for you to enter your pension reference.

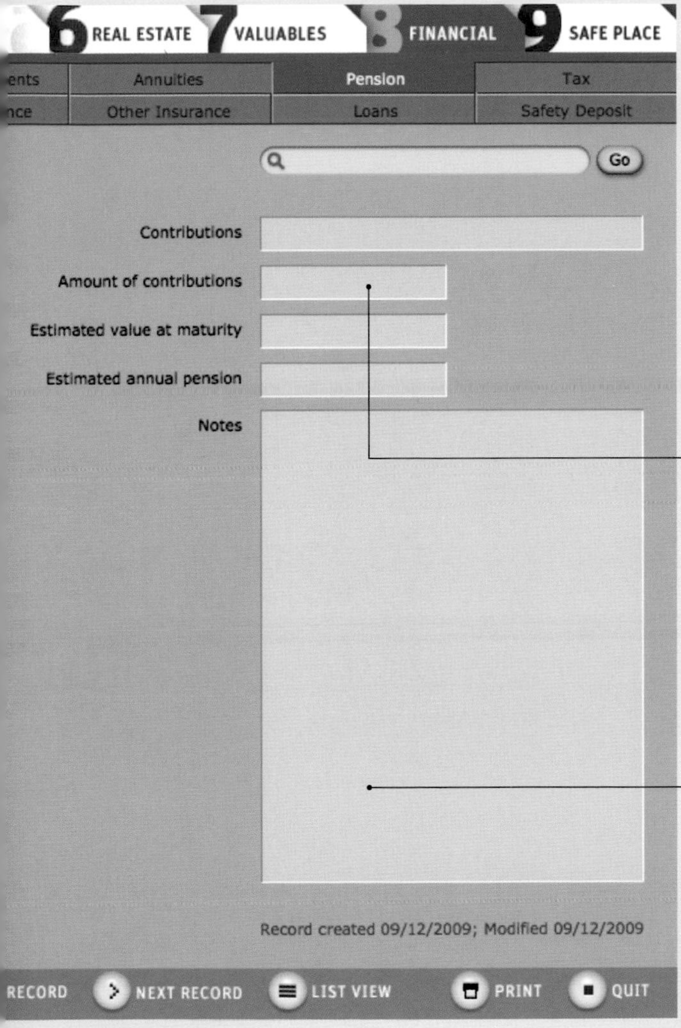

Amount of contributions Usually a set amount is deducted from your paycheck for investment in your pension plan, and often your employer will match your investment up to a certain percentage. If this is the case, be sure to include both of these in the total contribution figure here.

Notes Use this space to add any notes about the content of your pension; for example, if your plan invests in multiple funds, how you would define the investment mix, and whether it is slated as more conservative or intended for aggressive growth. (This kind of information can be found in your periodic statements from the investment company or on its website. See page 14 on Where to Find Records.)

8 FINANCIAL

Tax

This screen allows you to enter all the essential information related to your taxes. Because it is a multiple records screen, you can create separate records for different types of taxes, such as state versus federal, as well as for tax figures going back as many years as you choose.

Type of tax This is a drop-down menu providing different types of tax to select, such as city, state, and federal. If you would like to specify another, choose *Edit* to add a new type of tax to the list.

Tax payer ID number/IRS reference number If you need to discuss with the IRS any issues regarding taxes paid or owed, you will need to provide reference numbers, which can be entered here.

Charitable contributions/Health expenses Remember to add up all the money spent throughout the year in both these categories, because they may be counted as deductions.

Estimated payments If you are creating a record for the current year, it's a good idea to work out your estimated taxes in advance so you don't get an unwelcome surprise when it's time to pay. This is especially true if you are self-employed and don't have an employer automatically deducting taxes from your regular paycheck.

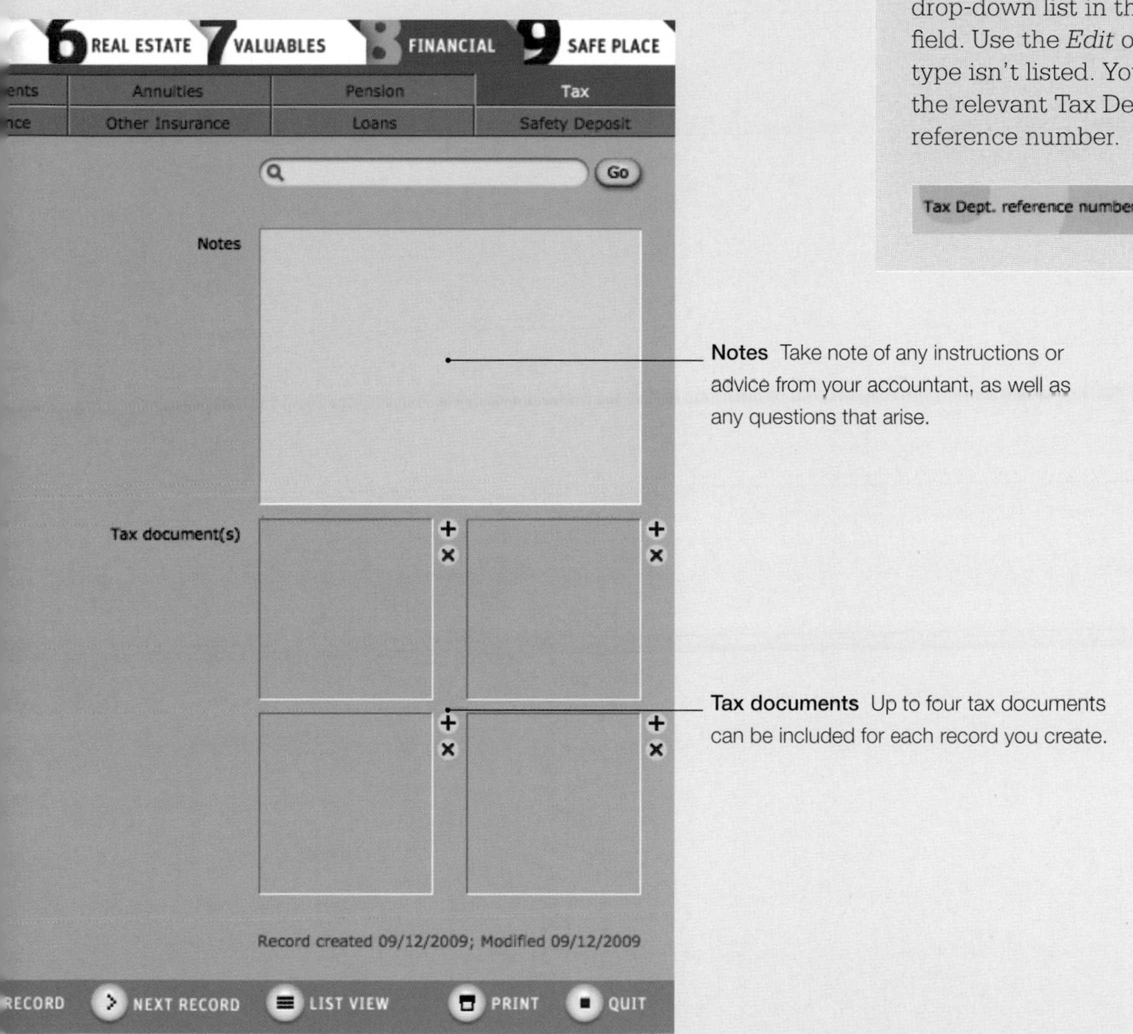

Regional Variations

You can choose the type of tax this record refers to by using the drop-down list in the Type of tax field. Use the *Edit* option if your type isn't listed. You can then add the relevant Tax Department reference number.

Tax Dept. reference number

8 FINANCIAL

Life Insurance

On this screen you can enter all the essentials of your life insurance. This is a multiple records screen, so if you own a few insurance policies, you will be able create a separate record for each one.

Life assured (insured) If this record is for your own life insurance (as opposed to insurance for a spouse, for example), click on the *Autofill* icon to automatically fill in your name.

Premiums/frequency To be sure you don't miss a payment, enter your premium amount and the frequency of payment required to maintain your policy.

1 FAMILY 2 MEDICAL 3 LEGAL 4 EMPLOYMENT 5

Stocks | Bonds | Mutual Funds | Ot
Life Insurance | Home Insurance | Vehicle Insurance | Tr

Life Insurance

Policy name
Life assured
Policy type
Policy number
Broker/adviser name
Broker/adviser address line 1
Address line 2
City/State
Zip/Country
Insurer
Insurer address line 1
Address line 2
City/State
Zip/Country
Premiums/frequency
Renewal date

Life insurance record no. 001 of 1

NEW RECORD DUPLICATE RECORD DELETE RECORD

Coverage includes Note the main points of your policy's coverage, as well as the names of designated beneficiaries.

Maturity date/maturity value If you own a policy that has a specified end date, rather than continuing indefinitely, add that date and the policy's corresponding value at that time.

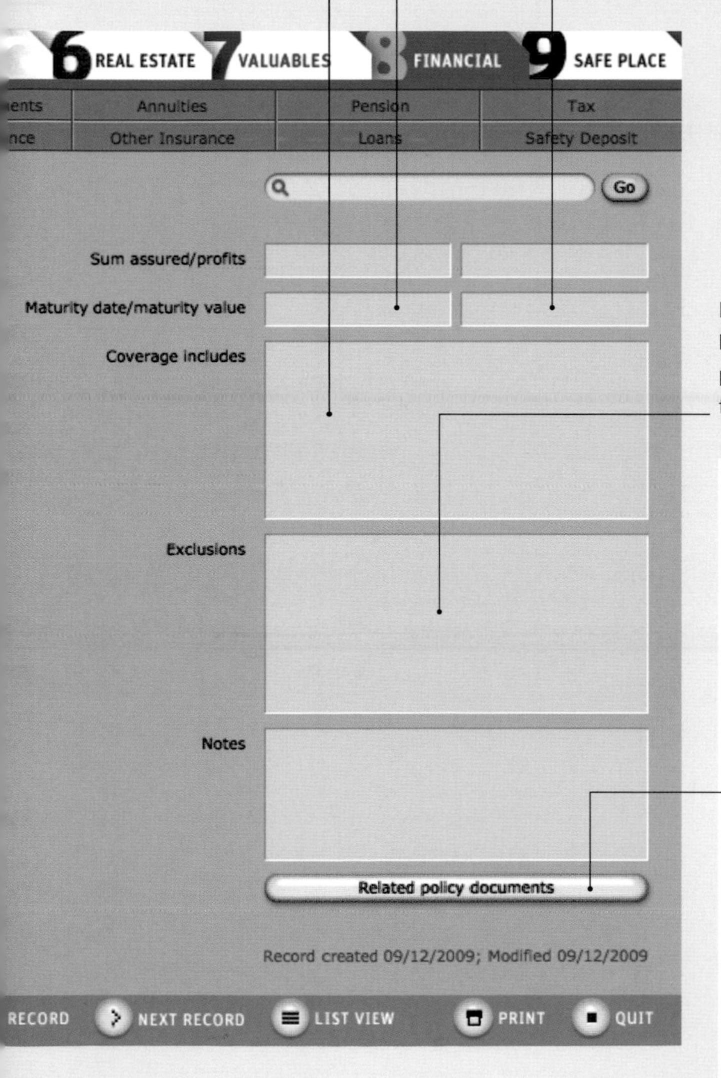

Exclusions If there are any limitations to the coverage provided by your policy, enter those here.

Related policy documents Clicking here will open a screen where you may upload up to five documents, such as your actual policy document or any follow-up reports from the insurance company, such as a change in premiums. To return to the full policy record screen, click *Back to policy details* at the bottom right of the screen.

8 FINANCIAL

Vehicle Insurance

All information regarding your vehicle insurance should be entered on this screen. If you have a number of cars or different types of vehicles, this multiple record screen will allow you to create a new record for each policy.

Vehicle type This field provides a drop-down menu of different vehicles to choose from. If yours is not on the list, click *Edit* to add your particular vehicle.

Policy type This drop-down menu offers several types of vehicle insurance, from third party to general accident. But if none of these match your policy, click *Edit* to add a new one.

Insured address If the vehicle is insured in your name, click the *Autofill* icon to automatically enter your home address.

1 FAMILY 2 MEDICAL 3 LEGAL 4 EMPLOYMENT 5

Stocks | Bonds | Mutual Funds | Oth
Life Insurance | Home Insurance | Vehicle Insurance | Tra

Vehicle Insurance

Vehicle type
Vehicle description
Policy type
Insured address line 1
Address line 2
City/State
Zip/Country
Broker/adviser name
Broker/adviser address line 1
Address line 2
City/State
Zip/Country
Insurer
Insurer address line 1
Address line 2
City/State
Zip/Country

Vehicle insurance record no. 001 of 1

NEW RECORD DUPLICATE RECORD DELETE RECORD

6 REAL ESTATE 7 VALUABLES 8 FINANCIAL 9 SAFE PLACE

…ents | Annuities | Pension | Tax

…nce | Other Insurance | Loans | Safety Deposit

Go

…olicy number/claims phone line

Sum insured/renewal date

Premiums/frequency

…ther drivers or permitted users

Coverage includes

Exclusions

Notes

Related policy documents

Record created 09/12/2009; Modified 09/12/2009

RECORD NEXT RECORD LIST VIEW PRINT QUIT

Policy number/claims phone line Include your policy number and the claims phone line here for easy reference, in case you need to discuss your vehicle's eligibility for a claim.

Coverage includes List the types of coverage your policy includes, such as damage, accident, theft, and so on.

Related policy documents Click here to access the screen for uploading your policy documents.

8 FINANCIAL

Loans

If you have taken out a loan of any kind, enter the terms on this screen. It's very possible you have multiple loans—you may have bought a home or car while still paying off a college loan, for example—so add a new record for each.

Loan type From this drop-down menu you can select the type of loan, such as a bank loan or credit purchase. To add an alternative type of loan that is not shown, choose *Edit*.

Loan purpose Describe what the loan is paying for: property, education, and so on.

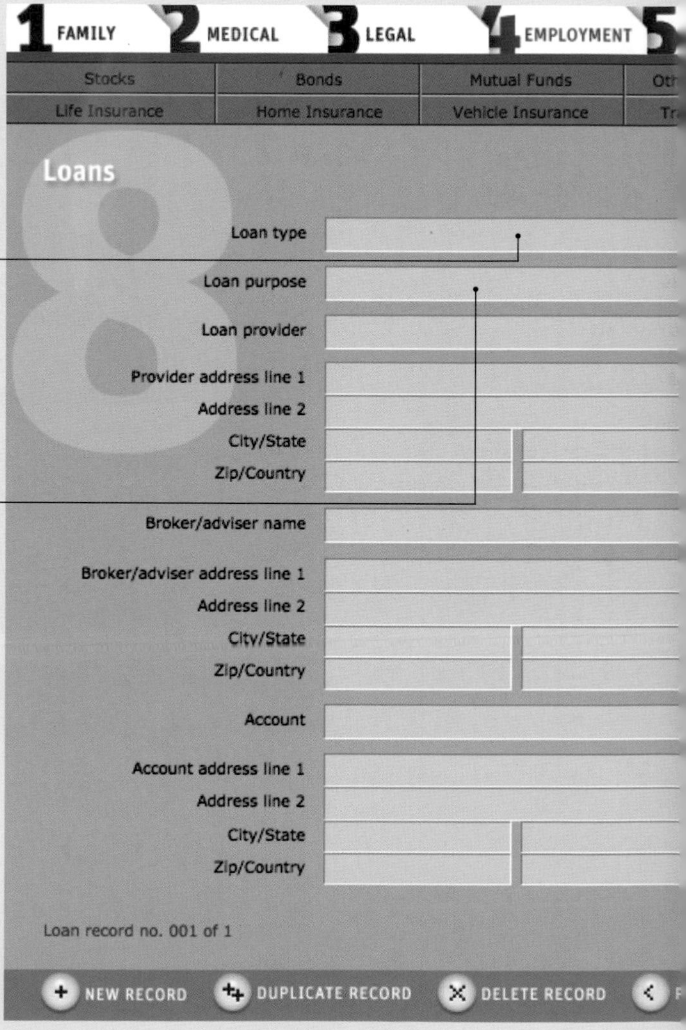

Loan amount/term Many loans are commonly long term, such as a 30-year mortgage. Enter the full amount of your loan and the length of time allotted for payment.

Interest rate Are you paying a fixed rate on your loan or does it vary over time? Enter the interest rates you have agreed to pay here.

Notes If any special terms are stipulated in your loan agreement, include them here. If you have refinanced your loan, you might note the change in terms from your previous agreement.

Loan documents You may upload two documents relating to your loan. If your loan has been refinanced, you might include both the original and revised loan documents for your reference.

Safety Deposit

If you keep your valuables in a safety-deposit box, this is the screen where you can enter the specifics. If you have multiple safety-deposit boxes—perhaps in multiple locations—you can create a separate record for each by using the *New Record* button.

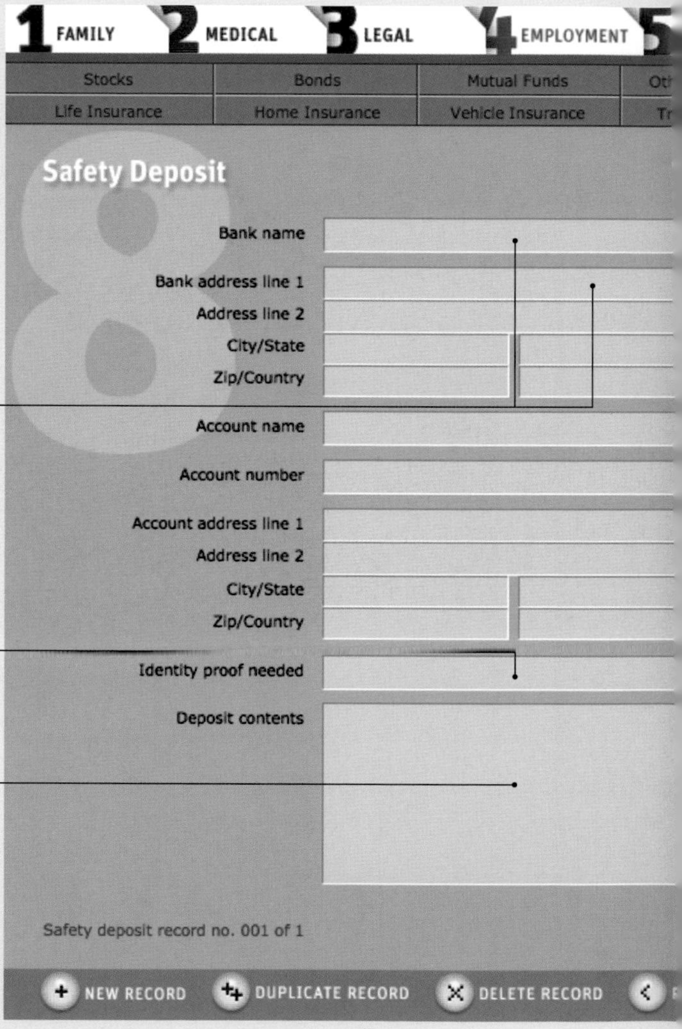

Bank name and address If you have safety-deposit boxes in more than one location, be sure to specify the bank's name and address where different items are stored.

Identity proof needed If your bank requires any particular documentation before allowing you to access your safety-deposit box, note that here.

Deposit contents List the contents of your safety-deposit box, so you always know the precise location of your valuables. You could also enter these items in the Valuables section of the program, where you can go into greater detail about the item.

6 REAL ESTATE 7 VALUABLES 8 FINANCIAL 9 SAFE PLACE

ents | Annuities | Pension | Tax
nce | Other Insurance | Loans | Safety Deposit

Go

Notes

Record created 09/12/2009; Modified 09/12/2009

RECORD NEXT RECORD LIST VIEW PRINT QUIT

Notes If appraisals have been made, you might want to enter the value of items stored. If you have removed any items from your safety-deposit box, make a note of that as well.

Bank Accounts

The Safe Place opens with a screen for your bank accounts. You will be able to enter all the key information needed for standard transactions as well as online banking. If you have multiple accounts—whether different types or at different banks—create a separate record for each one.

Account type This drop-down menu allows you to specify the type of bank account, such as checking or savings. To add a different type of account, choose *Edit*.

1 FAMILY 2 MEDICAL 3 LEGAL 4 EMPLOYMENT 5

Bank Accounts | Credit Cards | Website Passwords | e-mail Accou

Bank Accounts

Account type

Account name

Account number

Bank name

Bank address line 1

Address line 2

City/State

Zip/Country

Bank routing or transfer number

Branch phone number

Branch e-mail

Bank website http://www.

Online banking login http://www.

Username

Password

Bank accounts record no. 001 of 1

NEW RECORD DUPLICATE RECORD DELETE RECORD

Account name If this is a private account of your own, click on the *Autofill* icon to automatically enter your name. If you share an account, for example with a spouse, be sure to enter both your names.

Bank routing or transfer number If you send or receive wire transfers, this is an important number to keep on file.

Branch e-mail Enter your branch's e-mail address and click on the *E-mail* icon to automatically send a message.

Bank website Type in the web address of your bank here, and click on the *Web* icon to open the web page in your Internet browser.

Online banking log in If you enter the address of your log in page, clicking on the *Web* icon will immediately take you to that page so you can access your account.

Username and Password Use these fields to record the username and password you use to access your online banking facilities. Remember that these may be case sensitive, so be sure to enter them correctly.

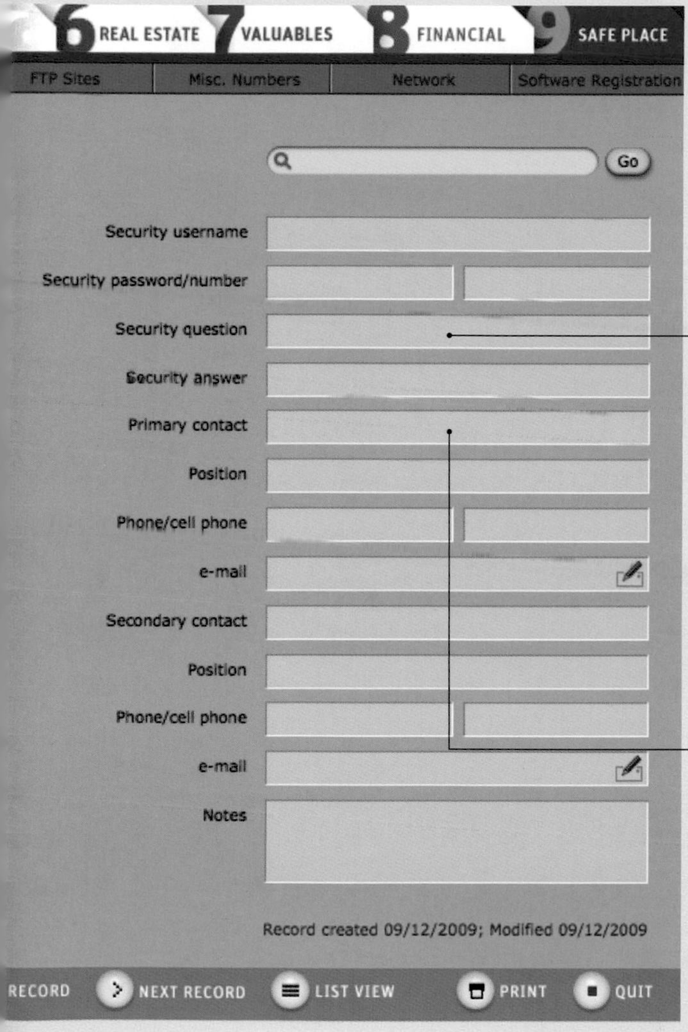

Security question Your bank usually requires you to keep a security question (and answer) on file. This drop-down menu features common questions, such as your birthplace or your first pet. If the question you use is not on the list, click *Edit* to add it to the options. You can also include the answer in the Security answer field below.

Primary contact and secondary contact If you have a primary contact at your bank, input the details here: name, position, contact telephone numbers, and e-mail address. If you have a backup contact, in case of emergencies, enter their details as well. To send a message to either, click on the *E-mail* icon at the end of the relevant field.

Credit Cards

In this record, you may add the details for your credit cards. You may have a range of cards affiliated with credit-card companies, banks, retail stores, and so on, so use this multiple records screen to create an individual record for every card you use.

Card type This is a drop-down menu listing types of credit cards, including those issued by different credit-card companies, as well as the various types of cards they offer, such as the American Express Green and the American Express Gold. If you don't see your card on the list, click *Edit* to add it.

Cardholder If you are the cardholder, click on the *Autofill* icon to fill in your name automatically.

Billing address Click on the *Autofill* icon to input your home address automatically, if this is where the card is registered.

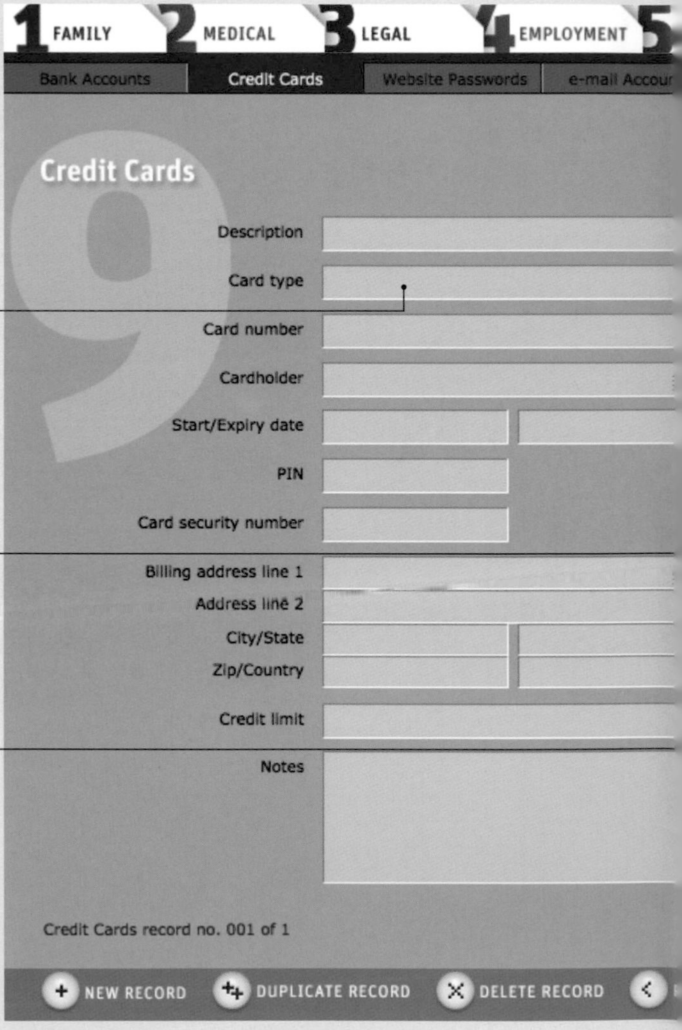

6 REAL ESTATE 7 VALUABLES 8 FINANCIAL 9 SAFE PLACE

FTP Sites | Misc. Numbers | Network | Software Registration

Go

Issuer name

Issuer address line 1

Address line 2

City/State

Zip/Country

Phone (billing/lost card)

Phone (fraud)

Issuer website

Website http://www.

Website login http://www.

Username/password

Security username

Security password/number

Security question

Security answer

Record created 09/12/2009; Modified 09/12/2009

RECORD NEXT RECORD LIST VIEW PRINT QUIT

Phone (billing/lost card) Be sure to find out the phone numbers both for billing and lost cards. If you notice your card is missing, you'll want to call and report this right away.

Phone (fraud) Enter the phone number for credit-card fraud—if your card is stolen, you'll want this number to be easily accessible.

Website To view your card company's website, input the web address and click on the Web icon.

Website log in If you have set up an online account for your credit card, enter the website's log in address and click the *Web* icon to go directly to the log in page.

9 SAFE PLACE

Website Passwords

Chances are you have accounts with numerous websites, whether you purchase goods at online retailers, subscribe to online publications, belong to social or business networks, or simply pay monthly bills. This screen allows you to document all your user names and passwords, with the multiple records screen enabling you to create a record for each site you visit regularly.

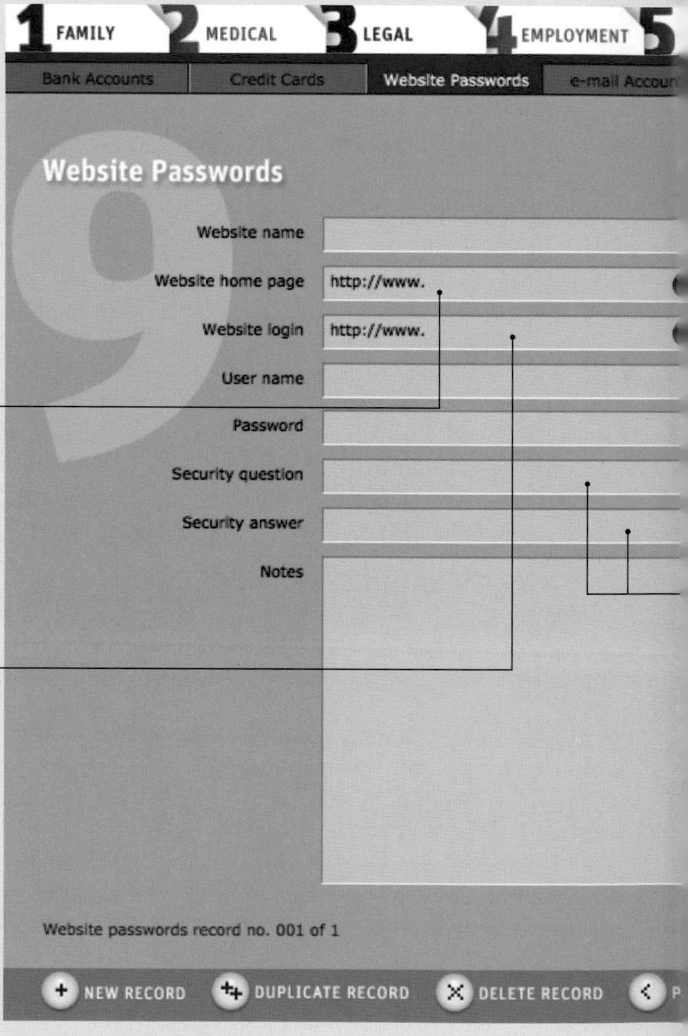

Website home page Enter the address of the website and click the *Web* icon to open the home page in your web browser.

Website log in Once you have entered the address for the website's log-in page, you can click the *Web* icon at the end of the field and you will be taken directly there.

Security question and Security answer
This question provides a drop-down menu listing potential security questions: You may enter the relevant answer in the Security answer field.

9 SAFE PLACE

E-mail Accounts

If you have multiple e-mail accounts, whether for business or personal use, you may create a separate record for each one on this multiple records screen.

Account description Use the description field to identify the e-mail account: personal or business, for example, or a Yahoo, Gmail, or Hotmail account. You can also use this field if you are entering details of someone else's account, such as another family member.

E-mail address Enter the e-mail address here and click the *E-mail* icon to send a message to that account.

Account type This is a drop-down menu listing different types of e-mail account, such as IMAP and POP. The company that hosts your e-mail account will be able to tell you which one applies to you. If yours is not listed, choose the *Edit* option to add it to the list.

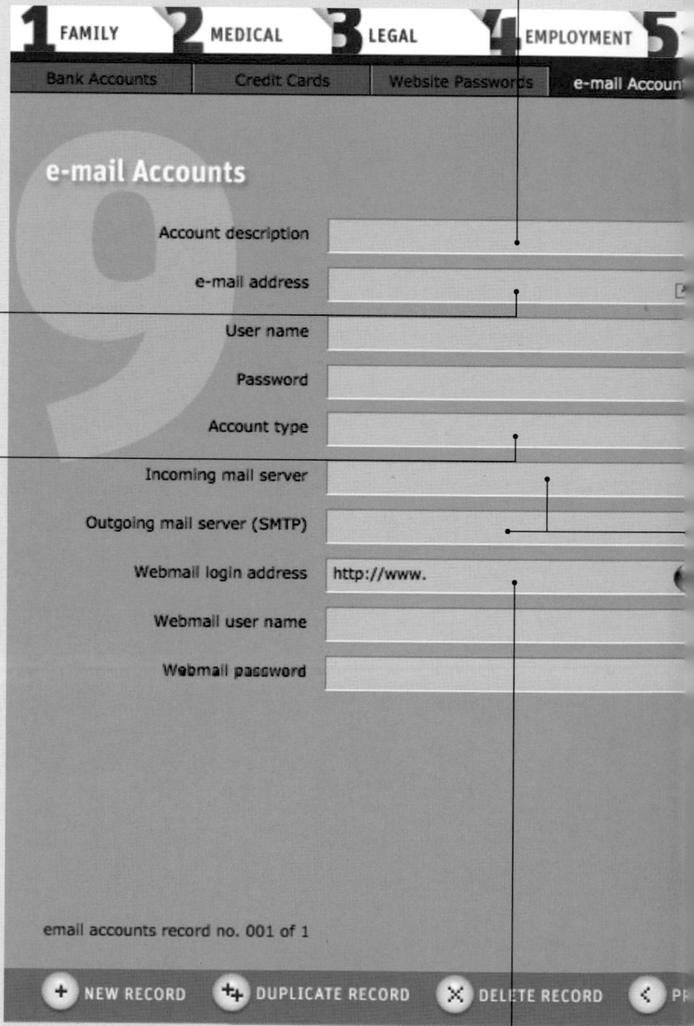

Webmail log in address If you have a webmail account (Yahoo, Gmail, or Hotmail, for example) that you access using your Internet browser, rather than through an e-mail program, you can enter the webmail log in address here. The *Web* icon will automatically open up the log in page.

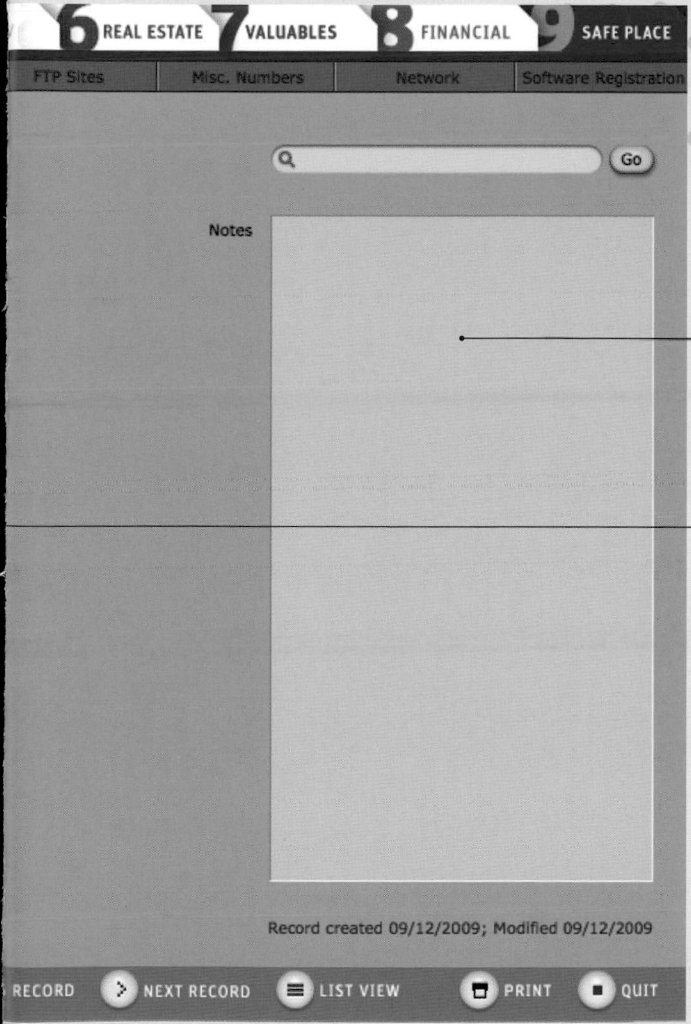

6 REAL ESTATE 7 VALUABLES 8 FINANCIAL 9 SAFE PLACE

FTP Sites | Misc. Numbers | Network | Software Registration

Go

Notes

Record created 09/12/2009; Modified 09/12/2009

RECORD NEXT RECORD LIST VIEW PRINT QUIT

Notes If you have designated different accounts for specific purposes, make a note of that here.

Incoming mail server and Outgoing mail server (SMTP)
The details you enter here are the settings used by your e-mail program (Entourage, Outlook, or Mail, for example) to send and receive e-mails. They can usually be found in the account settings of your e-mail program or from the company that hosts your e-mail account. It is useful to have these on hand in case you have a problem with your e-mail and need to reinstall your e-mail application.

9 SAFE PLACE

File Transfer Protocol Sites

If you use a File Transfer Protocol (FTP) site to send and retrieve large files on your computer, you can record the settings needed to connect to it on this multiple records screen. If you use more than one FTP site, you can create a record for each of them.

Name Enter the name of the person or company to whom the FTP site belongs.

User name and password If you are given access to an FTP site that belongs to an outside source—such as your employer—be sure to obtain the correct user name and password so you can log in.

1 FAMILY 2 MEDICAL 3 LEGAL 4 EMPLOYMENT 5

Bank Accounts | Credit Cards | Website Passwords | e-mail Accour

FTP Sites

Name

Host address (URL)

User name

Password

Security

Protocol

Type

Notes

FTP record no. 001 of 1

NEW RECORD DUPLICATE RECORD DELETE RECORD

Security This is a drop-down menu listing various FTP security options, such as KClient and GSS. If the FTP belongs to an outside source, you will not necessarily have—or need—this information.

Protocol This drop-down menu offers a variety of protocol options such as FTP (File Transfer Protocol) and SFTP (Secure File Transfer Protocol), among others. These are the sets of rules used by FTP sites so different computers can communicate with each other across a network. The person who hosts the FTP site will be able to tell you which one is appropriate for that site.

9

SAFE PLACE

Miscellaneous Numbers

If you have additional numbers that you need to keep in a safe place, you can list them here. These could include the code to a safe in your home, a file cabinet at work, an external storage unit, or maybe even a combination padlock for your bicycle or suitcase. This is the place for any numbers you might forget and need to record a security number for future reference. If you have a home-security system, the *Code* button on the Property Locations screen in Real Estate brings you here to enter your security code. Because this is a multiple records screen, you can add as many numbers as you need, so there's no end to the data that can be recorded.

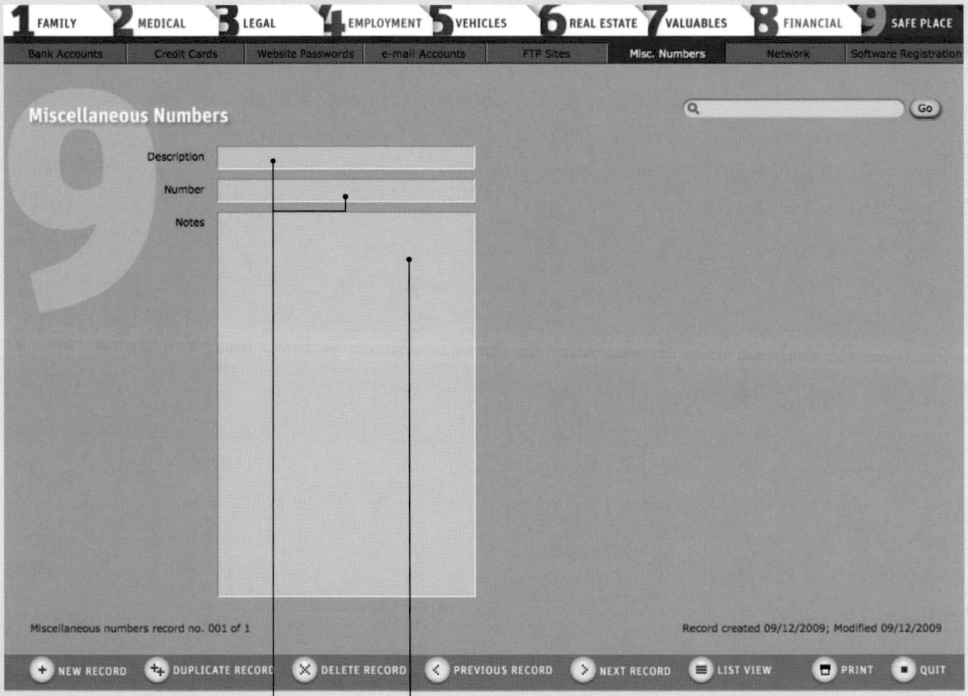

Description and Number Start by entering the item or location that relates to the number you are entering, and then input the number itself.

Notes Use the *Notes* field to specify any particular instructions for your personal numbers, as well as the locations where you use them. If you are the only person who knows where a certain locked item is found, for example, you will want to document its location in case you forget. If you have shared these numbers with anyone else, you might make a note of this, too.

Network

If your computer functions as part of a network—at a business, school, or home—you can enter the details here. This is a multiple records screen, so you can create a separate record for each networked computer.

This record page asks for a lot of technical-sounding information about your network, but the main thing to remember is that what these terms relate to is not of great importance here. For the database, you just want to be sure you have a record of your NetBIOS name, for example, but this does not necessarily mean you need a full understanding of what it is and what it does: You just need the information itself in case you have a problem with your network and need to reenter this information.

If you established the network yourself, you will know where to find all the details to fill in this page of the database. However, if the network was set up by somebody else on your behalf, you can still find the majority of the settings by following the steps on the following pages.

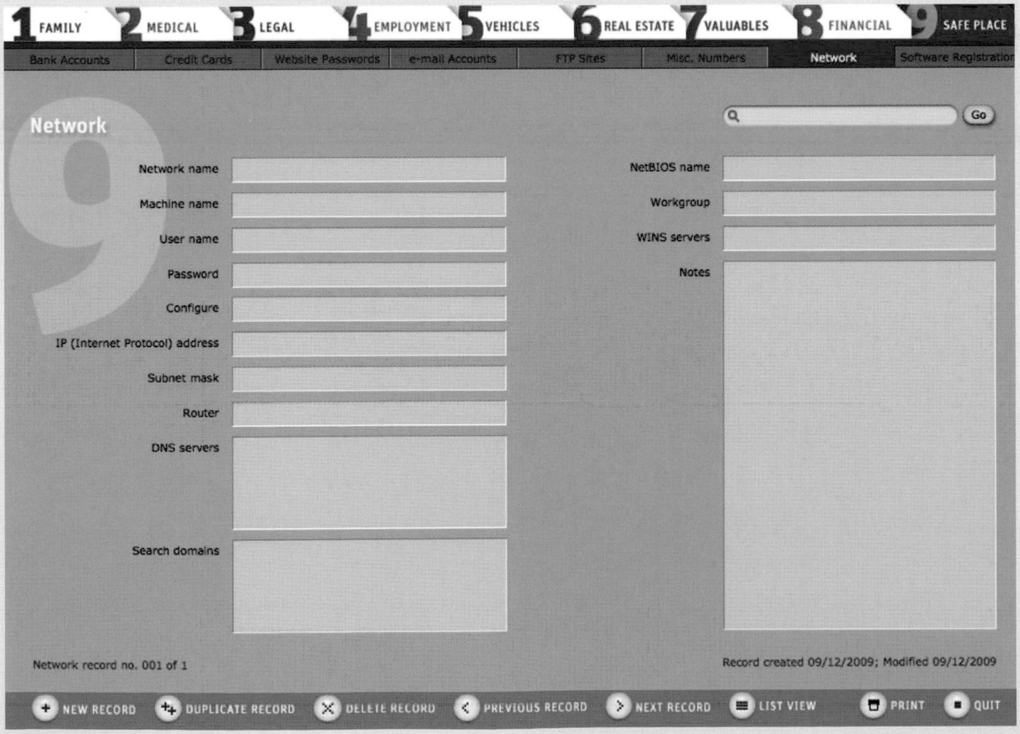

Network Settings in Windows 7

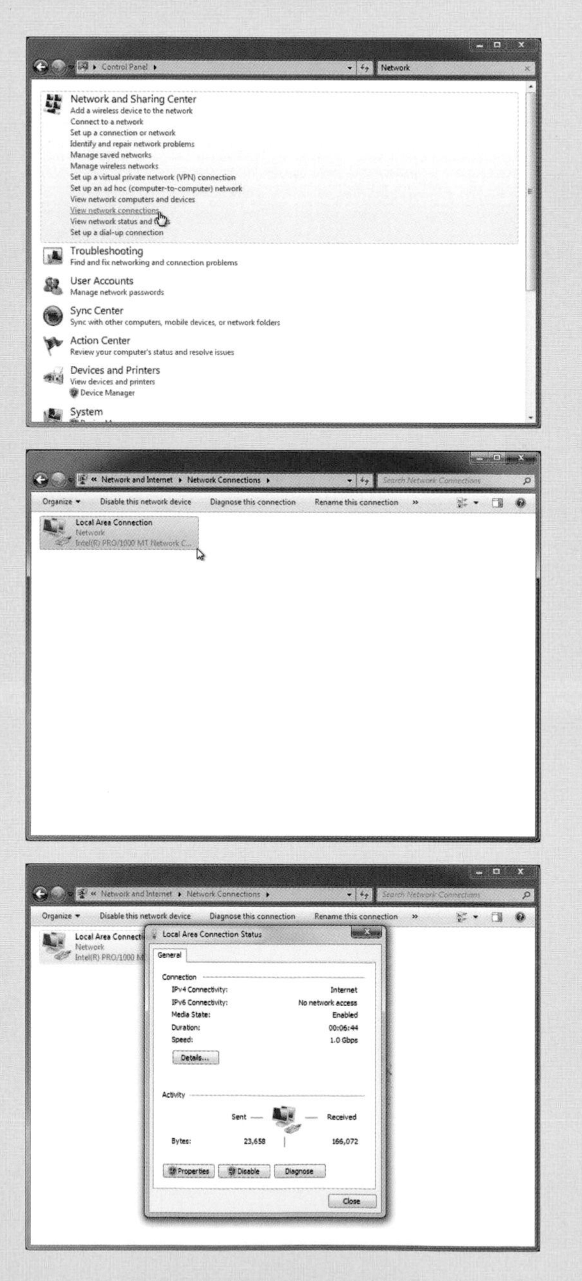

1 Click on the *Start* button at the bottom left of your desktop and choose *Control Panel*. Type "Network" into the *Search* box in the *Control Panel* window and select *View network connections* from the search results.

2 Select your active network and choose *View status of this connection* from the top menu of the window. (Note that you may need to click the chevron (>>) on the menu to see this option.)

3 When the status window opens, click *Details* to see your network settings. This is the information you will need to copy into your Network record.

Network Settings in Mac OS X

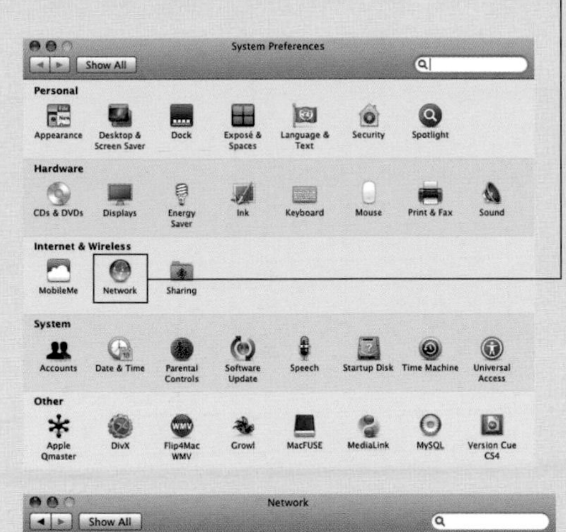

1 On a Mac running the OS X operating system, open *System Preferences* (usually located in your *Applications* folder) and choose *Network*.

2 A new window will show your network and its various settings. To see more information, click on the *Advanced* button at the bottom right of the dialog box. However, before you do, it is a good idea to click the *Lock* icon at the bottom left of the window, to be sure you do not change anything by accident.

3 You can now use the tabs toward the top of the *Advanced* settings window to see information about your network, such as your computer's NetBIOS name.

Software Registration

If you purchase software, you will have to input registration information when installing it onto your computer. This screen lets you keep a record of software-specific details, such as the serial number and activation code, as well as contact information for the software publisher in case you need to contact them for help or to upgrade. Each time you add new software to your system, remember to create a new record for it using this multiple records screen.

Version Most software has a version number. If you want to upgrade, knowing which version you are currently using is often essential.

1 FAMILY 2 MEDICAL 3 LEGAL 4 EMPLOYMENT 5

Bank Accounts | Credit Cards | Website Passwords | e-mail Accour

Software Registration

Product name
Version
User name
Serial number
Activation code
Purchase type/date
Publisher
Publisher address line 1
Address line 2
City/State
Zip/Country
Helpline
Publisher e-mail
Publisher website home page http://www.
Home page http://www.

Software record no. 001 of 1

NEW RECORD DUPLICATE RECORD DELETE RECORD

User name, Serial number, and Activation code If you need to reinstall your software, it is likely you will be asked for this information in order for it to work properly, so be sure to make an accurate note of each in these fields.

Helpline Enter the telephone number of the publisher's helpline in case you need to speak with a customer-service representative.

Publisher website home page/Home page Enter the web addresses of the publisher and the software. If you are looking for additional information regarding your software or other products from the same publisher, you can click on the *Web* icon to be taken to the relevant web page.

Publisher e-mail Enter the publisher's e-mail address and you can click on the *E-mail* icon to send questions or comments, without having to search for their contact details.

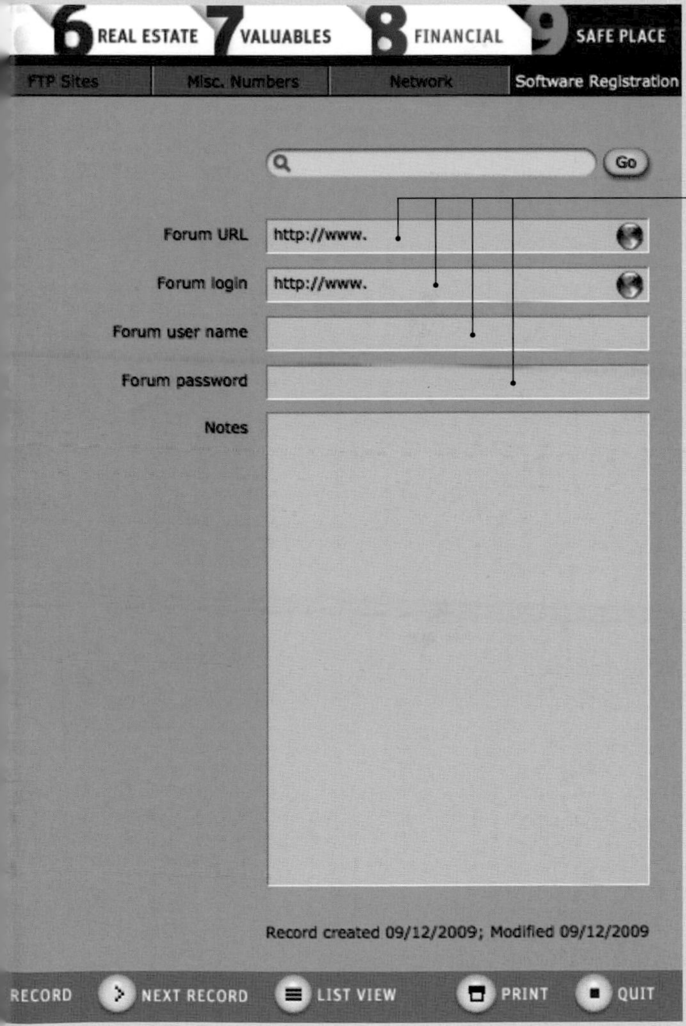

6 REAL ESTATE 7 VALUABLES 8 FINANCIAL 9 SAFE PLACE

FTP Sites | Misc. Numbers | Network | Software Registration

Go

Forum URL http://www.

Forum login http://www.

Forum user name

Forum password

Notes

Record created 09/12/2009; Modified 09/12/2009

RECORD NEXT RECORD LIST VIEW PRINT QUIT

Forum URL/Forum log in/Forum user name/Forum password If you participate in an online forum, enter the home and log in addresses (URLs) in the Forum URL and Forum log in fields. You can also enter your Forum user name and Forum password in the fields below. When you want to go to the forum, use one of the *Web* icons to open your web browser at the relevant page.

MEDICAL
LEGAL
5
6
VEHICLES
REAL ESTATE
8
9

RESOURCES

- TROUBLESHOOTING GUIDE
- GLOSSARY

To help you overcome any problems you might encounter while using the database, this chapter features a convenient troubleshooting guide, as well as an extensive glossary of computing terms, so there's always somewhere to turn if you get stuck. You'll also find some useful advice on copying the data from one computer onto another one if you upgrade either your computer or operating system.

Troubleshooting

No matter how much you try to avoid it, things can go wrong with computers from time to time. While every effort has been made to prevent this from happening with *Organize Your Life,* it is a computer program, and things can sometimes go wrong.

Some problems might only manifest themselves when you upgrade to a future computer system, but the following pages highlight some of the most common problems you may encounter—along with some helpful solutions.

General FAQs and troubleshooting

Q How come nothing happens when I put the disc into my computer?

A When you insert a CD into your computer, it will take several seconds before anything happens. This is because disc drives take a few moments to spin up to speed. If you use a Mac, a disc icon will appear on the desktop, but a window will not appear. This disc icon can be very easy to miss, especially if you have a cluttered desktop or have windows obscuring the desktop, so be sure to check it again.

If you are using a Windows computer, the disc uses the AutoPlay feature. You can disable it, which means you'll have to locate the files yourself, using the method on page 30.

If your computer is not recognizing the disc at all, try ejecting it and reinserting it. Inspect the surface of the disc for damage and try cleaning it using a lint-free cloth. Always wipe CDs gently, from the center outward.

Q Is it possible to use the program directly from the CD?

A *Organize Your Life* is on a prerecorded disc, so it's important that you install it on your computer's hard drive before you begin. Although it is possible to run the program from the CD, it will not save any new information, so anything you add would be lost when you quit the program.

To copy the program onto your computer, follow the installation instructions for your computer system: pages 30–31 for a Windows PC, and pages 32–33 for a Mac. This copies all the files you need from the CD to the computer's hard drive so *Organize Your Life* can run without the disc. In addition to saving your records as you work, running the program from your hard drive will also be a lot quicker than trying to run it from the CD.

Q I have accidentally installed the program for the wrong country. Can I change it?

A If you have installed the wrong regional variation of the program, simply follow the instructions for removing the program from your computer as explained in the computer-specific FAQ and troubleshooting sections on page 166. This will prevent you from having two versions of the program on your computer. Once you have removed the incorrect version of the program, you can reinstall the correct version. However, if you have already started filling in your records, keep in mind that removing the program from your computer will also remove all the data you have entered.

Q I'm trying to print a PDF, but why does only the first page appear?

A As mentioned on page 45, when you import a multipage PDF document into your records, only the first page will be visible and printable. To print out the full document, you will need to locate it on your computer's hard drive and open it using a PDF viewer, such as Adobe Reader.

Q I've entered a lot of information in a Notes field, but only some of it prints out. Why is this?

A Some fields in the database allow you to enter as much text as you like, which you can then scroll through when you are viewing the record. However, when you print a page, only the text that is visible on screen will be printed.

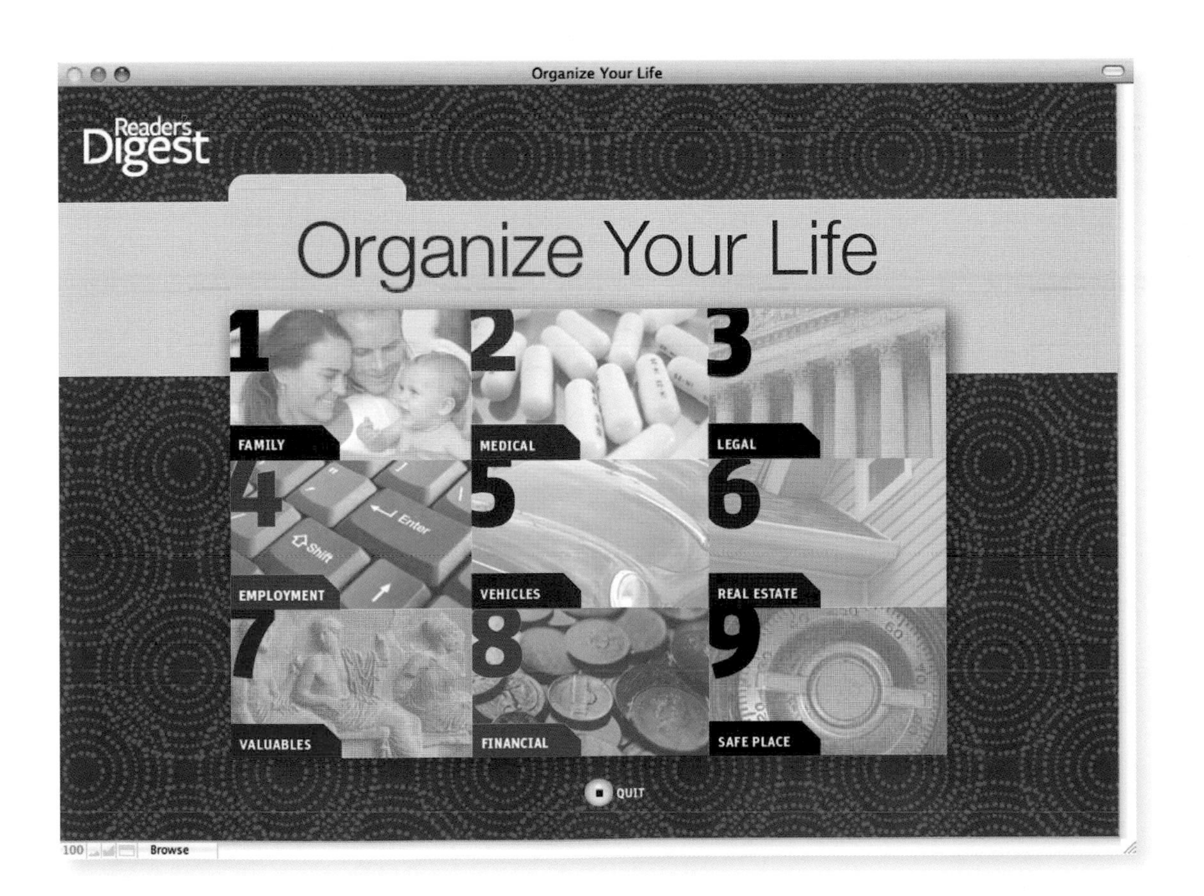

Windows PC FAQs and troubleshooting

Q I have installed the program, but why can't I find it on my Windows computer?

A The program will be added to the *Start* menu along with your other programs when you install it. If you cannot see it right away in the *Start* menu, click on *All Programs*. The program is stored within a directory next to a tool to remove the program, if necessary.

Q How do I remove Organize Your Life from my Windows computer?

A If you want to uninstall the program from your PC, click *Start* and go to the program folder in the *Start* menu. You will find an automatic uninstaller program that will delete the program and any information that you added to it.

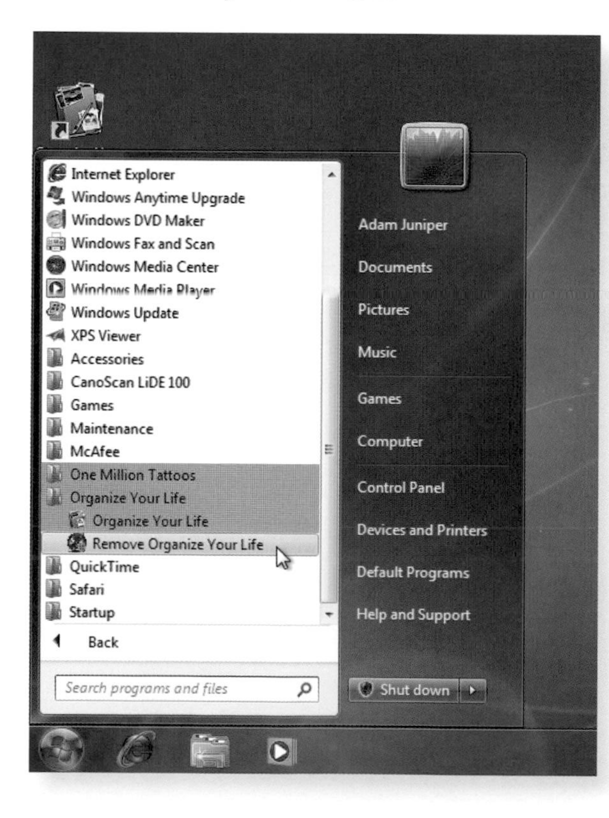

Apple Macintosh FAQs and troubleshooting

Q I cannot find the program on my Mac.

A On an Apple Macintosh your programs are all installed into the *Applications* folder on your hard drive. After following the instructions on page 32, you will find *Organize Your Life* within your *Applications* folder. The database is inside the program folder. Double-click on it to launch it.

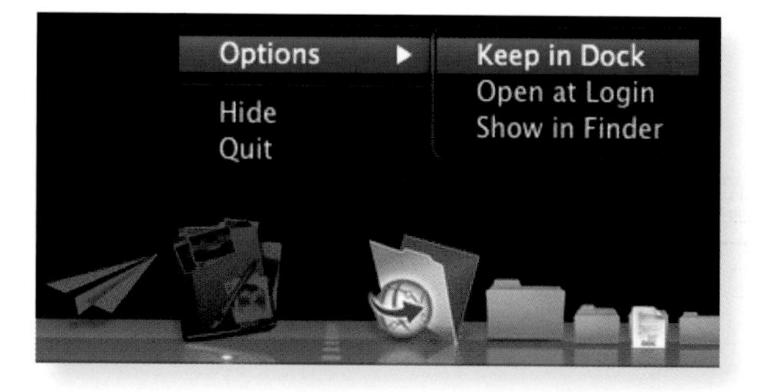

Q I would like to make the database easily accessible by using the dock on my Macintosh computer. Is this possible?

A Yes. Launch the program from the *Applications* folder as described above, then press Ctrl and click on the program's icon in the dock. Choose *Keep In Dock* from the pop-up menu. Now when the program is not running, you will see the program's icon in the dock, and you can launch it with a single click.

Q How do I remove Organize Your Life from my Macintosh computer?

A If you want to uninstall *Organize Your Life* from your Mac, open the *Applications* folder and drag the entire program folder from the *Applications* folder to the trash. However, be aware that this will also delete all the data you have added to the program.

Online help

Computer operating systems are constantly changing and being updated, so while every effort has been made to ensure that *Organize Your Life* runs smoothly on a wide range of computers, the future may bring new technical issues that cannot be foreseen.

However, if you encounter a problem that isn't covered here, there is an online resource that is fully updated with the latest information. To access this, open the database program and choose *Help>Frequently Asked Questions*...from the top menu. This will take you directly to the appropriate webpage for your country's program.

If you are having trouble accessing the online help pages from the program, use the URLs shown below.

Help
Search
Frequently Asked Questions...
Reader's Digest Website...

Organize Your Life Online Help
http://www.web-linked.com/RD_OYL/OYL_US/Organize_Your_Life_US.html

Organize Your Life FAQ

You're probably here because you've bought the Reader's Digest book *Organize Your Life*. While we hope that you'll find all the answers to your questions within the pages of the book itself, because of the way the internet works this page gives us the opportunity to provide up-to-the minute information. With computers constantly updating themselves, and new operating systems and upgrades coming out all the time, it makes sense for us to have this channel of communication.

Will Organize Your Life work on Windows 7?

Yes, Organize Your Life is fully compatible with the new Windows 7, as well as earlier versions Vista and XP.

I have installed the program, but I cannot find it on my Windows computer

The program will be added to the Start menu alongside your other programs when you install it. If you cannot see it straight away in the Start menu, click on All Programs. The program is stored within a directory next to a tool to remove the program, if necessary.

How do I remove Organize Your Life from my Windows computer?

If you want to uninstall the program from your PC, click Start and go to the program folder in the Start menu. You will find an automatic uninstaller program that will delete the program and any information that you added to it.

I cannot find the program on my Macintosh computer

If you installed the program as directed in the book, you will find it inside the Applications folder, in a folder called Organize Your Life. However you can install the program anywhere you like on a Macintosh computer, so it's possible you saved the file elsewhere and forgot it. In that case, click on the Spotlight logo (loupe icon) in the top-right of your Mac's desktop and type Organize Your Life into the search field.

Online Help Address

Type this address into your internet browser to access the Online Help directly:

United States: http://www.web-linked.com/RD_OYL/OYL_US/Organize_Your_Life_US.html
Canada: http://www.web-linked.com/RD_OYL/OYL_CAN/Organize_Your_Life_Canada.html

Index

A

About This Mac 20
accountants 15–16, 90
Acrobat Reader 24
Activation Codes 160
adding images 44–45
adding the archive 53
adjusting contrast 23
Adobe Acrobat Reader 24
Adobe Photoshop Elements 22
allergies 12, 76
Annuities 124–25
antiques 7
appliances 115
Applications 34–35, 53
archival media 52
artifacts 25
attorneys 82, 86
Auto Club Membership 97
Autofill 39, 66, 104, 124, 130, 132
automatic backup 57, 59
AutoPlay 31, 164
Autos 98–100
avoiding phishing 17

B

bachelor's degrees 69
backgrounds 61
backing up 50–59, 145
bank accounts 12–13, 15–16, 48, 60, 144–47
bank routing/transfer numbers 146
bar exams 69
basic search 46
beneficiaries 84–85
bills 10, 14, 110
black and white 19, 61
blogs 69, 71
Blu-ray drives 50
boats 100, 102
bonds 120–21
branch e-mail 146
broadband 58
building warranties 106
Burn 51, 53
business e-mail 68

C

C: drive 55
cable 12, 14, 110
Canada 64–65, 81, 94, 127, 164–65, 167
car modifications 99
cars 14, 98–99, 102, 105
cartridges 61
Caution 145
CD-ROM drives 28, 30–33, 50–52, 59, 145
cell phones 66, 74, 111
Certificates of Deposit 124
certification 69
changing passwords 37
charitable contributions 128
checking spelling 49
city tax 128
claims phone lines 135, 138
Close 45
closing the program 50
closing sessions 52
codicils 84
college degrees 69
color 19, 61
compatibility 52
compression 25
computers 7, 10, 28–30, 33, 43–44, 46, 48, 50–53, 56, 59, 61, 145, 154, 157, 164, 166–69
condensing search terms 49
conserving ink 61
contrast 22–23
contributions 127
copies 50–52, 60
CPUs 29
crashing 43
Create New Fill or Adjustment Layer 23
creating taskbar shortcuts 35
credit cards 12–13, 15, 48, 144, 148–49
cropping 19
current employment details 88–91
current employment status 92–93
current medications 76
current shareholding 118

D

D: drive 52
database 10–12, 17, 24, 30, 34–35, 38, 41, 43–44, 46–53, 65–66, 116, 144, 157, 165, 169
date formats 65–66, 94
default paper size 61
defensive driving classes 96
deleting records 40
Detect Separate Items 21
Devices 20
diagnoses 78
dietary requirements 77
disc storage 52
discs 50–52
divorces 84–85, 124
Dock 20, 35
doctorates 69
doctors 12, 14, 16
documents 10, 18–20, 22, 30, 44–45
dpi (dots per inch) 19
Driver Profile 96
driver's licenses 96
driving offenses 96
drop-down menus 41
Duplicate Record 40, 43, 70
DVD drives 50–51

E

E: drive 55
Edit 41
educational qualifications 68
Eject 52
electricity 12, 14, 110, 115
electronic documentation 45
Elements 22
e-mail 17, 39, 66, 68, 71, 82, 146–47, 152-53, 160
emergency contacts 67
Employed 88
employment records 13
employment types 88
entering passwords 37
eSata 56
essential computer terminology 29
exclusions 131, 133, 137
external hard drives 33, 56–57, 59, 145

F

Fabric Description/Brands 112
Facebook 66, 71
family data 13
Family Members 70–71
family records 42, 70
FAQs 164–69
federal tax 64, 128
fields 11, 64
file size 25
file types 19, 21, 24–25
filing 10, 14, 46
filing cabinets 10
final salary 95
financial records 13, 15–16, 118–43
financial section 12
Finder 53
finding records 14–15
fires 7
FireWire 56
flash memory sticks 54–55
floods 7
floor plans 113
formatting discs 51
Forum 161
FTP sites 154–55
Full Record 41

G
garages 105
gas 12, 14, 110, 115
Gigabytes (GB) 28–29
Gigahertz (GHz) 28–29
green + icon 44

H
hackers 59
hard drives 10, 28, 30, 44, 55–57, 145
Health Benefits 92
health expenses 128
health insurance 64–65, 80–81
helplines 160
home insurance 132–33
home phones 66
hospitals 74

I
ibackup.com 58
icons explained 39
ID (identification) numbers 11, 100
Image Capture 20
images 44–45
important documents 7
incorporated business owners 91
Individual Retirement Accounts (IRA) 126
ink 61
insert blank discs 51
inserting USB stick 54
installation 30–34
Installer Program 31
insurance 98, 130–39
interest rates 141
Internet phone ID 66
investments 15–16, 118, 122–23
IRS numbers 128

J
jewelry 7
Job/Business Description 90
JPEG files 19, 21, 25, 44

K
Keep in Dock 35
key database terminology 10
kitchen profiles 114–15

L
landscape format 61
launching the installer 30
launching the program 35
lawyers 14, 16, 69, 82
Layers 23
lease details 105
legal contacts 82–83
legal records 13, 47, 86–87
Leopard 56
Levels 23
license classes 96
license points 96
life insurance 12, 130–31
Like a USB Flash Drive 51
limited liability company owners 91
List View 40–41, 71, 73, 79, 82, 89, 94, 107, 121, 124, 138
loans 140–41
locate the program 52
locating files 35
log-in details 144, 146, 149–50, 152
lossy compression 25
lost cards 149

M
Mac OS X 20, 28
MacBook Air 28, 33
Macs 20–21, 28, 34–35, 53, 55–57, 159, 164, 166, 168–69
mail servers 153
marriage status 67, 71
masters degrees 69
maturity 120, 131
Medical Contacts 74–75
medical degrees 69
medical records 12–13, 16–17, 42, 65, 78–79
medication 76, 78
memory 28
military service numbers 68
minimum requirements 28
miscellaneous numbers 156
missing records 16–17
mortgages 106
motorcycles 100, 102
multisession 51
mutual funds 120–21
My Picture 67

N
names/addresses 10, 66, 70, 104, 142, 146, 148, 154
naming discs 51
navigation 38–41, 108
NetBIOS names 157, 159
Network 157–59
New Record 40, 43, 70, 72, 74, 94
New Scan 18–19
Next Record 40–41
nonsensitive information 59

O
oil 12, 14
online backup 58–59
online help 167
Open Finder 53
Open Folder 54
opening databases 34–35
opening folders 51
opening the license agreement 33
optical media drives 50–52
optimizing scans 22–23
OS X 56

P
paint colors/brands/finishes 112
paper sizes 61
paperwork 7, 10, 12, 46
passports 14, 68, 72
passwords 17, 36, 38, 108, 144–46, 150–51, 154, 168
PDF files 19, 21, 24, 45, 81, 165
peace of mind 7
pensions 12, 15–16, 126–27
personal data 66–69, 132
personal documents 72–73
personal e-mail 66, 71
personal legal data 84–85
personal medical profile 76–77
personal medical records 78–79
personal websites 69, 71
phishing 17
phone numbers 10, 66, 74, 82, 108, 110–11, 138, 147, 149
photographs 7, 10, 18, 20, 22, 30, 45, 67, 71, 83, 101, 105
Photoshop Elements 22
physician direct line 74
physician specialty 74
pipework 111
pixels 29
plumbing 111
policy documents 81
policy numbers 98
policy renewal dates 80
policy restrictions 80
political affiliations 69
postal code 65
power outlets 113
ppi (pixels per inch) 19
premiums 130, 133
preparation 30, 51
prescriptions 12, 17, 78

previous employment records 94–95
Previous Record 40–41
Print 40, 45, 60–61, 67
printers 28
printing records 60–61, 67, 145, 165
private medical care 64
processors 28
professional qualifications 69
profile page 66
prognoses 12, 79
Program Files 51-52, 168
property kitchen profiles 113–15
property locations 156
property profiles 104–5, 115
property room profiles 111–13
property utilities 109–11
property utility locations 107–9
provinces 65
provincial tax 64
purpose of residence 104

Q
qualifications 68–69
Quebec 64, 127
Quit 40

R
reusable drives 51
rewriteable discs 51
real estate 13–14, 104–15, 122, 156
record ID numbers 11
record screens 40
records 11–17
records at a glance 13
Recycle Bin 34
red x icon 45
Region 31–32
regional variations 64–65, 81
Related Policy Documents 131, 133, 135
relationships 70
remote computers 58
Remote Disc 33
Remove Safely 55
removing desktop shortcuts 34
removing files 45
renewal dates 96, 98
replacing files 45
residence 14
Results 47
retirement benefits 92
Revenue records 90
room usage 112
RVs 100

S
Safe Place 13, 37–38, 46, 48, 60, 108, 144–61
safe searching 48
Safety Deposit 142–43
salary/employment records 89
saving files 24–25
saving ink 61
saving records 43
Scan to Field 21
scanners 28
scanning 18–23, 44
screen resolution 29
Search 46–49
searching databases 46–49
searching for dates 48
searching shortcuts 49
security 7, 17, 36–37, 48, 59–60, 101, 108, 116, 144, 147, 151, 155–56
Self Employed 90, 126
serial numbers 115, 160
Series 7 69
service providers 58–59
service schedules 99
setting passwords 36
shortcuts 34–35, 49
Site Plan/Floor Plan 109
Skype phones 66
Snow Leopard 20
social networking sites 66
Social Security 126
software 58–59
software registration 160–61
spelling 49
Spotlight 20
Start Menu 34–35
starting salary 95
state tax 128
states 65
stockbrokers 69
stock purchases 119
stock sales 119
stock holdings 91
stolen valuables 7
storage 7, 52
storing records 12–13
storing references only 44
straightening images 22
subcategories 11, 42
surgeries 74
symptoms 78
System Preferences 57
system requirements 28–29

T
taxes 12, 15, 64–65, 90, 128–29
telephone 12, 14
Term/Maturity Date 120
terminology 11, 29, 64
Time Machine 56–57
title deeds 106
travel insurance 136-37
triggers 76
troubleshooting 164–69
trucks 100
trust funds 85, 124

U
union membership benefits 93
United States (US) 64–65, 81, 94, 126, 164–65, 167
universal health care 64
Untitled Disc 53
USB sticks 54–55, 59, 145
user names 146, 150, 154
utility records 10, 60, 108–11, 115

V
valuables 13, 116–17, 138, 142
vehicle documents 102–3
vehicle insurance 134–35
vehicle records 13, 96, 100–101
Version 160
viewing images 44–45
viewing search results 47
Vista 28

W
wallcovering description/ brands 112
warranty details 98
Web icon 39
websites 17, 58–59, 69, 71, 110, 144, 146, 149–51, 160, 167
wills 84–86
Windows 7 19, 28, 35, 50
Windows 7 Backup and Restore 56
Windows Explorer 31, 51–52, 54–55
Windows Fax and Scan 18–19
Windows PCs 18–19, 28, 30–31, 34, 50–51, 56, 158, 164, 166, 168–69
Windows XP 28, 51
wizards 57
write once 51

Z
zip code 65
zoning information 109